BEGINNINGS

BEGINNINGS

Thomas C. Hunter

THOMAS Y. CROWELL, PUBLISHERS
Established 1834
New York

BEGINNINGS. Copyright © 1978 by Thomas C. Hunter. All rights reserved. Printed in the United States of America. No part of this book may be used or reproduced in any manner whatsoever without written permission except in the case of brief quotations embodied in critical articles and reviews. For information address Thomas Y. Crowell, Publishers, 10 East 53rd Street, New York, N.Y. 10022. Published simultaneously in Canada by Fitzhenry & Whiteside Limited, Toronto.

FIRST EDITION

Designed by Eve Callahan

Library of Congress Cataloging in Publication Data

Hunter, Thomas C
  Beginnings.
  1. United States—Biography. 2. Professions—United States. I. Title.
CT220.H86   920′.073   77-27831
ISBN 0-690-01687-5

78 79 80 81 10 9 8 7 6 5 4 3 2 1

To Joanne, Kathleen, Alison, and Susan—in their beginnings.
And especially to Pat.

Contents

Acknowledgments

Had it not been for the enthusiastic response of playwright Richard Bruner, with whom I initially discussed the concept behind *Beginnings*, I might never have pursued it. I am grateful to the persons I interviewed, who gave so much of their time and of themselves, and to my wife and daughters for their patience.

There are many others whose assistance and encouragement made the book possible, especially Hugh Rawson, editor at Thomas Y. Crowell, Publishers. My thanks to Anne Anderson, Duane Anderson, Alan Bell, Alvinia Bridges, David Galligan, Thomas Greene, Wendi James, Marie Kaspar, Matthew Kaspar, James Kiernan, Katie Kiernan, Ann Laffey, Michael Laffey, Peter Lassally, Andrew Maguire, Patricia Murray, Thomas Murray, John O'Connor, Beatrice O'Rourke, David Parks, Ede Robinson, Louis Sica, Wayne Smith, Ray Stricklyn, David Swindells, Sue Swindells, and Ann Whitestone.

BEGINNINGS

Beginning of Beginnings

For a period of more than a year, extended because of the difficulty of getting to people with extremely heavy schedules, I spent hundreds of hours in interviews and follow-up conversations and correspondence with the twenty-four people in this book—men and women who have distinguished themselves in a great variety of fields. I traveled approximately 10,000 miles and met with them coast to coast to learn the stories of their beginnings.

I sought the answer to a problem posed by someone who once said to me, "Every person grows up with some kind of dream, but it seems most of them don't achieve it. At some point they give up, let loose, and lose it. The average person just wakes up one morning and says, 'I'm nowhere. I didn't do what I wanted to do. I was a kid with a dream, but all of a sudden I'm not a kid anymore. I'm not going to make it.'"

Each interview was a learning experience. I asked about the ways in which careers got started. I asked about "heroes" and role models who influenced career decisions, events and circumstances which channeled interests, career options not pursued and why not, underlying personal motivations, key turning points, and sources of major satisfaction.

Responses were candid. The people were not only willing but eager to share their experiences and insights. Walter Cronkite had to delay the start of our interview to place a quick call to Washington for information from Vice-President Walter Mondale's office bearing on a story which had broken late the night before. Still, he gave more than an hour—his agreed-upon time for uninterrupted, thoughtful reply to questions about his beginnings. Choreographer Ron Field delayed a rehearsal for a Bette Midler television special to elaborate on points he especially wanted to make. Harry Mullikin, president of Western International Hotels, chose to arrive late for an important business dinner rather than rush his responses.

As interviews added up, patterns emerged. One was universal: all subjects still were occupied with strong interests from their youth—and in most cases never had diverted from them.

The most apparently clear-cut career change was Roberta Flack's switch from teaching to singing—but her only major interest always was music, the subject she taught. Attorney F. Lee Bailey once considered a writing career, but among the books he read as a youth was one by a lawyer which "intrigued" him, and in his career as an attorney he has written fifteen books himself. Although Mary S. Calderone did not embark on her full-time career until she was in her fifties, she now applies an early interest in biology and her studies in medicine to her work in human sexuality.

In most other cases the consistency is clearer. Novelist Bari Wood, who worked for a short while in theater, started writing her first novel as a child. Julian Bach was once a journalist and now is a literary agent, but his preteen interest in publishing is basic to both. The trend is still sharper with others. Academy Award-winning actress Louise Fletcher stayed hours at the first movie she went to alone and saw it over and over. From the seventh grade, columnist Erma Bombeck wanted to do nothing but write humor.

A determined pursuit of early interests marks the lives of all—both in the refining of skills and talents and in the seeking of opportunities to apply them—not so much in the interest of achieving success as for the sake of doing well in what each found fulfilling and satisfying.

In these pursuits there is a strong inclination to remain one's own person—almost to the exclusion of immediate consequences—and to adhere to personal principles. Inherent is a recognition of and certainty about one's abilities.

"There's one philosophy that has always prevailed through my career," says David Kennerly. "If you want me to work for you, you have to let me do it my way." Rosser Reeves recalls, "Along the way I got fired from two or three agencies because I wouldn't write advertising their way." And from Craig Claiborne: "I am self-willed. I do what I do the way I do it, and that's it."

Underlying these attitudes, though, is a thorough grounding in skills.

Kennerly: "I had a lot of self-confidence, but I really was winging it, hoping I wouldn't mess up. I knew the basics of what I was doing, but there was a big gap. I talked to people and watched how they did it."

Reeves: "It convinced me, I didn't know what I was doing and that, if I ever wanted to learn, I had better get myself to New York."

Claiborne: "The school was absolute paradise. The courses in cooking and table service were beautiful. I couldn't believe that I was learning such things, at such a rapid clip too."

Intensive preparation sometimes strained physical abilities to bring them in tune with inner desires. Such single-mindedness links the delicate art of ballerina Patricia McBride with the aggressiveness of baseball player Pete Rose.

McBride: "I cried a lot when I started lessons, because ballet was so difficult for me. My toes pointed in, although ballet later corrected that. I couldn't understand why I wasn't able to perfect the steps easily. . . . It took weeks and weeks of practice, but slowly I improved."

Rose: "I know I can hit, so when they switched me to third base in

May 1975 I spent all my time taking ground balls. Day in and day out, at age thirty-three, I took twenty-five to thirty minutes of ground balls before every game. A twenty-three-year-old kid could have gone out there and taken ground balls for an hour; I had to work so damned hard it tired me out."

Although many of the achievements of the twenty-four people in this book are impressive, they themselves are not larger than life. Like everyone else, they have doubts and questions too, but have been able to move beyond them. And that seems to be their identifying mark.

Walter Cronkite is refreshing—and encouraging—when he says, "I don't know why I'm a success—what that 'special' quality is. I watch myself on the tapes and think anybody can do a better job, and most of them can."

Erma Bombeck too says, "I don't know," and, reflecting on her career, adds, "This has opened a whole new world for me. I have found out things about myself—things I can do that I never dreamed I could do."

Harry Mullikin hints at an answer in relating that his oldest son, at a time when he was unsure of his own career goals, once told him, "I really hope I find something that turns me on as much as the hotel business turns you on."

The comments of the men and women in the following chapters do suggest an answer. Might it be so simple as that people can achieve if they can sort out what they really want to do, find the ways, and then just go ahead and do it?

The comments of these twenty-four men and women were made in response to specific questions. In order not to intrude, I have extracted the questions so that the people might share their thoughts and experiences directly with you, the reader.

Julian Bach

LITERARY AGENT

Julian Bach, who heads one of the largest and most prominent literary agencies, is a former foreign correspondent, author, and magazine editor. The agency, which bears his name and is based in New York City, where he was born, represents some five hundred American and British authors, including Theodore H. White, Judith Rossner, C. L. Sulzberger, Elliot Richardson, Susan Brownmiller, Jim Fixx, Robert Elegant, Thom Gifford, Jan Morris, and Sir Edmund Hillary. The agency has at one time had both the number-one fiction and nonfiction books on The New York Times *best-seller list. It also had five main selections of the Book-of-the-Month Club in a fourteen-month period and four of the club's featured alternates in a five-month period. Bach is a vice-president of the Society of Authors' Representatives.*

I did not consciously choose that, after almost twenty-five years as a writer and a magazine editor, I would become a literary agent. I just found myself no longer an editor in the late 1950s, and it all evolved from that.

It's marvelous to be in the kind of work you've always wanted to be in, that you feel at home in, and that you knew from your early years you were reasonably good at. I always was interested in the printed word, news events, journalism—publishing in its broadest sense. When I was twelve a classmate and I put out a little magazine for our elementary grade. We wrote jokes, bits of school news, and little pieces about our teachers. For covers we cut and pasted covers from the *Saturday Evening Post* and other magazines.

When I was thirteen I put out another magazine by myself. It could be a footnote in the history of nutty children. I was a serious collector of stamps, and I had a desire to become a big, powerful banker. So I named my little magazine "The Philatelist and Banker." It included stories about stamp collecting and banking news items I plucked from the financial pages of *The New York Times*. It was thirty pages long, and I had thirty subscribers—members of my family and parents of my friends—who paid ten cents a copy. I typed it all myself, using only two pieces of carbon paper—three hundred original pages with six hundred carbon copies. I charged ten cents for full-page ads and five cents for any smaller than that. I put out seven or eight issues, during which period I spent half my life at the typewriter. At the same time, I had my schoolwork, athletics, my social life, and my stamp collecting.

Work never has been a labor for me. About 80 percent of it is engrossing pleasure. My mother was an energetic woman who would have been very successful in business had she ever gone into it. She set high standards for whatever she did and worked hard at it. I picked up from her a sense of accomplishment from hard work. I liked hustle and bustle, and from the start I admired the people in

Julian Bach: It's marvelous to be in the kind of work you've always wanted to be in, that you feel at home in, and that you knew from your early years you were reasonably good at.

my family, who all were in business. My father and his brother headed the sales operation for a tobacco-growing business which had been in our family for two or three generations. They had a dozen tobacco farms in the Connecticut River Valley, but the headquarters were in New York City, where we lived. The business involved a great deal of traveling, however, and they finally sold it.

All my relatives were successful in business, including an uncle who was a banker, which accounted in part for my early interest in banking. Another uncle had a sizable mercantile business in Manhattan, and I worked for him during the summers when I was fifteen and sixteen. When I wasn't packing shipping crates I spent most of my time taking down and putting back sixty or seventy heavy ledgers with which the bookkeepers worked. That queered me for life for run-of-the-mill merchant business and made me well aware that I didn't want to be stuck in a business office—or a bank—when I was older.

I continued to enjoy writing, though, and I learned that people who do something well tend to do more ·and more of it. In prep school I wound up on both the newspaper and literary magazine at Choate, and when I got to Harvard I became an editor of the *Harvard Advocate*. I was reading a lot of different magazines too, and I always wanted to see with my own eyes what I was reading about. As this curiosity increased, it edged me more and more into the world of journalism, for you have no business in journalism unless you are curious. Uncurious people .tend to go in other directions.

My first summer home from college I contacted the late Bruce Bliven, the editor of the *New Republic*. Living in the Depression, I was aware of the growing labor movement and was tremendously interested in the social issues with which the magazine dealt. I explained to Bliven my interest in seeing firsthand what I had been reading about. He apparently liked my approach, because he invited me to his office. We met there for fifteen minutes one morning, and then he suggested we talk at greater length over lunch. A week later he gave me a dozen letters of introduction to important New Dealers.

With the entrée those letters provided, I visited scenes of violent labor strife that summer in North Carolina, Pennsylvania, and West Virginia. I went to isolated and primitive mining and textile mill towns and lived with miners and textile workers in their crowded shacks. It was 1934, and you couldn't have had any sympathy in your blood and not be aware of the terrible differences between people who still had money and the people you saw living in total, rotting poverty. When I went back to Harvard that fall, I wrote three articles, which the *New Republic* published.

When I graduated magna cum laude and Phi Beta Kappa from Harvard in 1936 with a degree in sociology, I had a partial scholarship to continue my studies at the London School of Economics. The prospect of living in London seemed a wonderful opportunity to prepare myself for any one of the three career interests I had by then—journalism, foreign service, or teaching. The British Empire still was a very powerful factor in the world, and were I to become a journalist with a serious publication, such work would involve world affairs and mean plenty of contact with the British. Or, if I went into the foreign service—diplomacy—the more I knew about Britain and the British the better off I would be. Or, if I went on to teach sociology, a master's degree would have been a necessity, because I was interested in teaching only at the college level. So there was everything to gain and nothing to lose by taking the scholarship, and fortunately my family was able to pick up the main part of the tab.

After four or five months in London, however, I simply woke up one morning and knew I wanted to be a journalist. I knew I wanted a mixture of the world of ideas, the world of people, and the competition of the marketplace, and journalism richly offered all three. I acted immediately, discontinued my studies, and began to make the rounds of the London bureaus of the major American news agencies and newspapers. I had some things going for me, since I had had an excellent education, had been involved in journalism since I was seventeen with school and college publications of high quality, and had been published in the *New Republic*. But I was a twenty-two-year-old ex-student vying for openings highly desired and sought after by experienced, professional journalists, and I had no success.

Eventually I wound up calling on small, feature news agencies along Fleet Street. Then I met Raymond Moley, who had been one of the chief New Dealers under Roosevelt. Moley recently had started a magazine called *Today*, and he offered me a modest retainer as a European correspondent. It was about enough to pay for breakfast, but it provided me with credentials, which was extremely important because I was able to pass myself off as an honest-to-God correspondent. You learn very quickly in life that the other guy makes assumptions; nobody had to know I was a journalist by the skin of my teeth.

I managed to write some stories from England, but it was the day of the great foreign correspondents and Europe was teeming with them because of Hitler and the developing situations which eventually led up to World War II. I didn't stand much chance competing for exclusives against veteran, by-lined writers from *The New York Times*, the Hearst papers, the Associated Press, and the like. So I decided to go where the big-shot correspondents wouldn't crowd me out, and I became the self-appointed correspondent for *Today* magazine in the Balkans. The other correspondents weren't there, because the Balkans were relatively unimportant.

When I arrived in Athens with my typewriter under my arm something happened which I hadn't expected but which proved very fortunate. The reaction of government officials and other important figures was, "My God, here's an American correspondent. Look, he has a typewriter. He has credentials. He must be a junior John Gunther. Have a drink. We'd be delighted to have you interview us." John Gunther, the chief correspondent for the Chicago *Daily News*, recently had published his great book *Inside Europe*, which established him not only in Europe but all over the world.

Very often—whether it was in Bulgaria, Rumania, Greece, Turkey, or Yugoslavia—people asked me, "Do you know John Gunther?" Knowing full well the intent of the question, I did not answer no, for I *once* had been introduced to Gunther at a party in London. We had shaken hands, said hello, and exchanged three or four words before he moved on. So without technically telling a lie, I could answer with gall, "Yes," and I did so—without elaborating further. The assumption that followed was, "This young American knows John Gunther personally. Of course we'll welcome him." As a result I got some very good scoops, not only for *Today* but also for a London-based feature agency with which I had a tie-in by then, and I also sold some pieces to *The New York Times Sunday Magazine* and *The Nation.*

It was all very heady and exciting for a twenty-two-year-old, especially in countries like Bulgaria, Yugoslavia, and Greece, which were under dictatorships and where I led two lives. During the day, I interviewed cabinet chiefs and prime ministers. At night I generally was "underground," interviewing Communists or anti-monarchists. On a number of occasions I was led through labyrinths of streets and alleys and in and out of houses and kitchens of restaurants—to be sure no one was following me—before coming face to face with leaders of the underground in secret places. In Yugoslavia I interviewed Vladimir Machek, the fine leader of the Croat Peasant Party, who was surrounded by no fewer than six heavily armed bodyguards, in a farmhouse about eight miles outside of Zagreb.

My Balkan career ended one night in a hotel room in Sofia, the capital of Bulgaria. I realized after six months that I just wasn't willing to pay the price eventually to become a top-drawer foreign correspondent with a by-line in one of the bigger newspapers or with my name on the masthead of a major magazine. I wasn't willing to spend ten years in small hotel rooms in foreign countries where I didn't speak the language, where I didn't have friends my age, and where I would have to learn two or three major languages fluently to avoid using interpreters. Also, the pull of New York was very strong. All my family and childhood friends were in Manhattan, and I had a girl who was at Smith. It might have been different had I come from a town I wanted to get away from, but to me New York was an attractive home base which offered a wonderful other life on top of my work. So I came home to the States.

The *Review of Reviews* magazine, which had bought many of my pieces, offered me a job as assistant foreign editor for about $40 a week. It was a good magazine, honored but fading with old age, and it folded eight months later. I then went to *Time* for a job. They looked me over with some care but didn't take me on. But they did refer me for a job which was open at *Fortune*. There were three finalists for a position as staff writer, and we each received an assignment to write. I believe I came in third out of the three, but *Fortune* referred me on to *Life*. Several editors interviewed me there, and while I was sitting with John Billings, the managing editor, he received a telephone call from the Time-Life bureau in Paris. The message was, "We have it!" *It* turned out to be the first pictures ever taken of the then largest single military secret in the world—the Maginot Line, the string of immense fortifications protecting the eastern frontier of France against Germany. Just overhearing such a scoop, I was ready to get down on my knees to ask for the job. Two weeks later *Life* hired me.

I was at *Life* from 1937 until I went into the infantry in 1942. During that period I held several jobs, including assistant foreign news editor. When I came back after the war, I returned to *Life* and stayed for another two years. Immediately after the war, Random House published my book, *America's Germany,* which gave American readers the first full picture of what the American occupation of defeated Nazi Germany was like. It was very well received, getting highly favorable reviews in both the daily and Sunday *New York Times. The New Yorker* gave it a cheer and commented on "the particularly easy-going writing style." Easy-going for the reader maybe, but I knew I had rewritten many parts six and seven or even eight times to end up with that "easy-going" tone.

I learned much at *Life* and enjoyed writing for the magazine, but thinking at age thirty-two about what had been a wonderful job at twenty-three I began to feel, "This is getting very repetitious. The news events are always different, but it's always foreign news." I think of that now whenever I go into Baskin-Robbins or Howard Johnson's. Sure, they have thirty-one flavors or twenty-eight flavors, but it's all ice cream. What difference, when you're scooping it, if it's chocolate or raspberry?

Variety is what I always have liked, and I felt I was going to trap myself at *Life*, where—as with any major magazine or newspaper—you become compartmentalized unless you are at the very top, and I had no reason to think that from among my peers—any one of whom was as good or better than I—I someday would be chosen managing editor. At about that time, Walter Lowen, a headhunter in the media field, told me the number-two spot, executive editor, was open at *True*, a Fawcett publication. It was the largest men's magazine in the world, with a circulation of more than two million. The job represented a step upward and, above all, an opportunity to break out of compartments. At *True*, almost everything in the magazine would be my concern. I applied for the job, got it, and was there four or five years, after which I received an attractive offer to become one of four senior editors at *Look*. I decided to accept, but when I went to the management at Fawcett to resign, they said, "We have been thinking of making you editor of *Today's Woman*." It was one of the larger women's magazines, and I had never been a full editor-in-chief. So I decided to stay with people who knew me and my work, rather than risk going to *Look* and finding out either that they might not like me or I might not like them.

When I joined *Today's Woman* I had no idea that General Foods, a major advertiser, had pulled its advertising out one month before I took over. The masthead billed *Today's Woman* as "the magazine for young wives." It was edited to appeal to women between the specific ages of eighteen and twenty-eight—a marvelous advertising market because those ages mean first husbands, first households, first babies, which in turn mean first furniture, first linen, first silverware, first everything. The problem was nobody could keep a woman who first subscribed to the magazine at age twenty-four from reading it at thirty-five, forty-five, and older. I remember a letter from one reader who wrote, "I'm a 63-year-old grandmother, but I feel young." But that was not the woman the publisher was trying to sell to the advertisers. So while circulation kept going up, advertising kept doing down. *Today's Woman* finally went out of business at the same time that the *Woman's Home Companion*, *Collier's,* and *The American*—all with larger circulations—also folded.

Shortly thereafter I took a vacation in England. While there, I met a most remarkable young man, and it was he who made a suggestion which bumped me into the literary agency business.

Christopher Shaw was twenty-one years old when mutual friends introduced us in London. He was in such a hurry to be successful that when he graduated from Eton he went straight into business instead of going on to Oxford or Cambridge. He borrowed money from classmates and friends and bought a small, failing feature agency in London which sold minor weekend features to British newspapers and magazines. In two or three years he rebuilt it into the biggest, or next to biggest—certainly the most thriving—feature agency in Britain. Christopher was a workhorse. Twelve-hour days, seven days a week, meant nothing to him. He would leave his office late on a Friday, heading for the airport in his chauffeur-driven limousine while he dictated letters by telephone to his secretary back at the office, and then catch an eight o'clock plane to Rome. He'd arrive in Rome and go to a party and sign Sophia Loren to a contract for her life story for newspapers and magazines all over the world. The next morning he would fly to Switzerland, rent a car, go see William Holden, sign him to a similar contract, and then fly back to England.

When I met him he said to me, "For all our growing success, we never have been able to sell anything in America. You seem to know a lot of people in magazines there. Would you become our New York representative?" I told him I would be willing to see what I could do with his very best material but that I wanted total veto over what he sent me and that I did not want to feel I was his New York representative. The first material was a ten-part series, designed to run in a British daily, by Graham Fisher, a British journalist who specialized in writing about the royal family. Fisher had a superb contact in Buckingham Palace—the Queen's personal footman. The Queen's footman is in a tremendous position to observe the royal family up close. He is one of only three servants who automatically accompany the Queen whenever she travels, and he stands immediately behind her chair at all meals, whether there are two, fifty, or a hundred guests.

The material was marvelous. It described how Prince Philip made his drinks, how the Queen and he entertained their personal friends, what they talked about between themselves, and among other things included many anecdotes about the Queen's personal dresser, who had been her governess and was so much at home with her that she was one of the few people in the world who could lose her temper with the Queen and get away with it.

Interest in the royal family was still widespread in America at that time, and there was a large market for such material, but no American magazine was going to publish ten short takes of 2,000 to 2,500 words each. So I sent them back to London with some editorial comments and suggestions and recommended that they rework them into three pieces of 5,000 to 6,000 words each.

I knew that the executive editor of the *Ladies Home Journal* was keen on the British royals, and I sold the revised pieces to her for $35,000—which would be more like $75,000 today. Shortly thereafter, I sold another major piece to *McCall's* for $15,000. Word of these two quick sales spread around London, and British authors and journalists got the ridiculous impression that there was a new literary agent in New York who was picking pound notes off the trees. I began to receive material from British writers, including some good ones—first a trickle, then a stream.

It wasn't that I then decided the literary agency life was for me, but I told my wife I would give it "six months" as an experiment. The first dozen clients I had were British, but within a short time the majority were American, and very quickly the biggest part of my activity came to involve books. The agency kept building and grew like Topsy, and I have been at it happily ever since.

F. Lee Bailey

DEFENSE ATTORNEY

First admitted to the Massachusetts bar in 1960 after graduating from the Boston University law school, F. Lee Bailey has achieved international prominence as defense attorney for such celebrated cases as Dr. Sam Sheppard, Dr. Carl Coppolino, the Boston Strangler, Captain Ernest Medina, and Patricia Hearst. Born in Waltham, Massachusetts, in 1933, he left Harvard, where he was interested in a writing career, to enlist in the military service in 1952. He served as a fighter pilot and legal officer in the U.S. Marine Corps, during which time he switched his career interest to law. He has maintained his strong interest in aviation, which, by his own admission, rivals that which he has for law. He is president of Enstrom Helicopter Corporation of Menominee, Wisconsin, and has logged more than 12,000 hours in flying various types of aircraft.

From the time I was very young—about twelve years old—until I was in the Marine Corps, I wanted to be a writer. I always got good grades in English, and I found writing easy to do. I was editor of my school paper at Kimball Union Academy in New Hampshire, and my curriculum, to the extent that there were electives, was heavily lingual—Latin, French, and English. I continued that at Harvard, where I majored in English.

Being able to write and speak the King's English is not as common in my profession as it ought to be. There are many lawyers who have great ideas but, being unable to express them, are ineffective whether it be at the trial level or the appellate level. I frankly am more comfortable with the business of articulation than many people are. I have sat in rooms and heard people peel off beautiful sentences in conversation, but if they march up to a public podium they have to have it all written out. Even in prep school I did fairly well in oratorical contests.

I had a lot of early interests—sports, automobiles, woodworking, boating. When I was in prep school I was the postmaster, and I remember the headmaster telling the student body, "I'm making Bailey the postmaster because he is very busy, and, if you want something done, give it to somebody who's already busy," which I suppose is true to a point. I got that from my mother, who was a very energetic person and able to accomplish a great deal.

At the end of my second year at Harvard I was perilously close to being drafted. Trench fighting was not my idea of a good time, so I decided to enlist in the service for flight training. It offered a good education, a good bed, and—for those who could qualify—a nice option to being drafted. I went through Navy flight training, which was an eighteen-month program, because the Marines didn't have their own flight school. I chose the Marines, though, because when I went through the service—it was 1952–55—they got the jet fighters. The Navy was getting piston-driven airplanes, multi-engine air-

F. Lee Bailey: *I don't think anybody really plumbs the depth of his self-reliance and ability to draw on his own resources in tight situations any more than he does when he is flying single-seat jets.*

planes, and helicopters. All the hot shots wanted to be Marines and fly jets.

Flight training was perhaps the best preparation I ever had for the practice of criminal law—in which, as a defense attorney, you can find yourself in some very lonely positions with the whole system lined up on the other side. I don't think anybody really plumbs the depth of his self-reliance and ability to draw on his own resources in tight situations any more than he does when he is flying single-seat jets. In flight training you learn early on that if you don't become completely self-reliant you're going to kill yourself. It's a trait that's especially important in criminal law, because there are too many easy outs you can take; too many temptations to fold your tent without exploring every angle. I have found that lawyers frequently become intimidated in this branch of the business. Sometimes you just have to irritate a judge or a prosecutor in order to service your client completely. A good degree of self-reliance and self-confidence is extremely helpful in such instances. Also, no one ever is going to try a case where he doesn't make some mistake somewhere along the line, and, if that shatters you, your efficacy is gone. I have seen it happen many times in the courtroom where a guy gets his foot in his mouth and is useless after that because he is unable to recover.

Meticulous preparation is critical too. I always have had a tendency to be thorough. The earliest evidence I have of that is when I worked on automobiles as a kid. I would put in a new part, look at the one next to it, and say, "Gee, that doesn't look very good." Pretty soon I had rebuilt the whole damn thing. I regard a lawsuit the same way. It's often the part you don't see at first which will win it for you. Once you get a case, whether the fees are there or not, there's only one way to prepare it, and that's all the way.

Law first intrigued me when I read a book by Lloyd Paul Stryker, who was one of the great trial lawyers of the 1930s, 1940s, and 1950s, but that didn't divert me from wanting to be a writer—primarily a writer of fiction, which is odd because I have fifteen books out and they all are nonfiction. My first real involvement with law came about in a curious way. I was assigned to a fighter squadron in Cherry Point, North Carolina, right after I got my wings. Everybody in the squadron had to have a ground duty. Mine was as second assistant legal officer. It was a nothing position, but ground duty was just a joke anyway. Unfortunately, one afternoon about a month after I got there, the first assistant was killed when his plane crashed. Almost immediately after that the legal officer's wife made him quit flying. So I suddenly acceded to the position. My commanding officer said to me, "If you want it, you're it." Nobody else really wanted it. It was a lot of work and was a duty looked on with disfavor in those days, but I liked it.

I started out as a prosecutor but very quickly shifted to defense. I sat as a member of the court, which is sort of a super-juror. Then I was promoted to a higher echelon, where I convened the courts on behalf of the commanding officer and supervised the operations of the courts. Frequently I had to sit in the back of the room and rule on objections by signaling the president with my thumb so that he would know which way to rule. The job really required a lawyer, but there weren't enough to go around. I also had an assignment as an investigating officer. That gave me a lot of experience in dealing with violent death. Our group had two thousand men in it, and I had to investigate every aircraft crash to determine whether or not it had occurred in the line of duty or due to misconduct, because the death benefits depended a lot on such determinations.

My military legal experience really was across the entire spectrum, and it intrigued me. As my interest grew, I began to work, when I was off duty, for the civilian lawyers whom I had first become involved with in connection with military cases. It was excellent experience, and if they had a trial going on I would take basket leave to work on it. I did investigative work for them and sat with them at the defense table in court. They advised me that that was the only way you could get to become a good trial lawyer, because law school gives you very little help in that regard. As I later learned, they were entirely right. It quickly became apparent to me, when I later did investigative work for lawyers while I was attending law school, that a lot of them never had any investigative training. They were putting their cases together in very clumsy fashion.

The lawyer I principally worked for in North Carolina was Harvey Hamilton, Jr. He offered to help me out with law school and give me a job as soon as I graduated. I didn't take the offer, because I didn't want to stay in North Carolina. So after I got out of the service I entered law school at Boston University. Because of my military experience and recommendations from my commanding officers and the civilian lawyers for whom I worked, the school waived the requirement for three years of completed undergraduate work. I had a tremendous advantage in law school because one of the majors in my squadron had been taking a LaSalle Extension University course in law. He wasn't the brightest fellow in the world, and I used to help him a lot. That fairly well forewarned me about what the courses would be like.

Law school involves a totally different philosophy of education than does undergraduate work. It can cause a real problem because first-year law students usually have to change their thinking—their whole approach to studies. It's all analysis and decisions, and the ones who don't make the transition usually flunk out. The first year, I went to every class and did all the homework. The second year, I spent about half my time in class. And during the entire third year, I don't remember going any more than ten times. I worked in law offices all through school—about sixty hours a week. People with outside employment had morning sessions, so we were through by noontime, and I would work until about eight or nine o'clock at night.

While I was still a student I went to a course for criminal lawyers. The lecturers were a lot of the top guns of their day—Jake Ehrlich, Percy Foreman, Grant Cooper. They all had different techniques, but when—simply by listening—you discovered common denominators and found that your thinking meshed with theirs, it was very encouraging. You got the feeling you were getting a handle on things. Jake Ehrlich, who is dead now, was particularly encouraging. We developed a relationship which stretched over several years, and he was most helpful in letting me bounce ideas off him after I began practicing law. His work, along with that of Edward Bennett Williams, became my index.

I graduated from law school in 1960 and passed the bar examination that December. By virtue of having tutored Ed Williams' babysitter, who also was a law student, I enjoyed having lunch with him the day after I took the bar examination. He was the first person I remember as someone I looked to as an ideal. In the 1950s he was the man. There was no question about that. He had all the hard cases and some remarkable results. I had no intention of going into criminal law, though. My dissertation, which was published when I was a senior, was on how to try a plaintiff civil case. I just happened onto criminal cases. They were the first ones to roll around.

The very first was a murder case which was getting a lot of attention in the newspapers. The defense lawyer, by putting his foot in his mouth, had invited evidence before the jury that his client had flunked a lie detector test. From my military experience, where lie detector tests were par for the course, and also because of six months I spent as a law student in preparing another case involving polygraph information, I knew as much as—if not more than—any lawyer in the country about how to cross-examine a polygraph examiner. So I got called in to work on the case. Then the defense lawyer, who was seventy-two years old, had a heart attack, and I wound up finishing it. It was just that coincidental. Hard on the heels of that, we had a whopper of a rape case in which we were going to establish the inadmissability of polygraph evidence. This was the case I had been preparing as a student. We never got to establish anything, though, because the defendant was acquitted, but the case made the front pages in the newspapers and led to a whole string of other criminal cases. The notoriety from the first two just catapulted me into the others that followed.

Law has been tremendously satisfying, although there was one point when I had more than a passing thought about getting out of it. It was when the Feds in Jacksonville, Florida, put me on trial for nine solid months on a charge of mail fraud. It was a godawful, dragged-out trial which bankrupted every defendant but me during the course of it. It was the worst thing that ever happened to me, brought about in part because I had recently published a book lambasting the postal inspectors as the largest group of idiots in law enforcement—which I thought was well documented, but they resented it. I finally was severed out of the trial, after which the government refused to go to trial against me alone. The case was dismissed.

The Sam Sheppard case in 1966 was my most noteworthy up to that point, because he was so far down at the bottom of the barrel when we got hold of him. He supposedly had lost every recourse and had nowhere to go. It took four years, but we finally won a reversal of his conviction for his wife's murder. The case of Captain Ernest Medina was another highlight because of its immensity, involving as it did the My Lai massacre in Vietnam. Also, it was a military trial, and I really prefer those. That was a case where everything worked the way it was designed to work. Usually the system is very frustrating—something is going wrong or somebody is twisting it. It always is satisfying to extricate from a sticky situation somebody who deserves to be extricated. It is never satisfying—though the public will never believe it—to extricate somebody you know damn well is going to be back.

Erma Bombeck

SYNDICATED COLUMNIST

*Erma Bombeck, from the time she was a young girl in
Dayton, Ohio, knew that she wanted to write humor and
pursued that goal all through high school and college.
Today, from her home in Paradise Valley, Arizona, she
writes a thrice-weekly newspaper column for the Field
Newspaper Syndicate. She also has written four books
and appears regularly as a humorist on the daily network
television show* Good Morning, America. *She is a member
of Theta Sigma Phi, which awarded her its Headliner
Award in 1969, and a member of the Society of Professional Journalists. Her book* Just Wait Till You Have
Children of Your Own *received the Obianna Award as
the best book of humor in 1972, and in 1973 she received
the Mark Twain Award as the top humorist in the
country.*

From about the seventh grade on I knew exactly what I wanted to do. I wanted to write, and I wanted to write humor. I never, never wanted to do anything else. That can be both a blessing and a curse. I don't know what would happen if someone picked out an area with such singleness of purpose and then didn't fit in.

I don't know if people are born with a sense of humor or develop it for some particular reason, but mine has been there for a long time. My family laughed a lot, and maybe that rubs off. Someone asked my mother once if she had a great sense of humor, and she said, "I had her, didn't I?" I guess I go back to that.

In the early 1940s, at a time when everybody else was cutting out Queen Elizabeth paper dolls and reading Nancy Drew mysteries, I was reading Robert Benchley and James Thurber and H. Allen Smith. I got an education out of them. There also was a woman named Catherine Brush who wrote a humor column. She must have been syndicated, because we used to get her in the Sunday paper. I would read her and think, "Oh, boy." There was a lot of humor around at that time. I think it really flourished then.

I worship at the feet of Benchley. He had a quality of putting himself down, and I loved it. I don't know if there are any psychological ramifications, and I don't even care. But if I can laugh at myself and not offend anybody, that's the route I want to go. Benchley did a funny thing about a cruise where he put on his white suit too early in the spring—when no one else was wearing one— and he felt as though a big spotlight was following him around. He did that sort of thing better than anyone. I like self-effacing humor. I call it the loser's syndrome. Around supermoms I used to feel twenty pounds overweight.

For Christmas I listed the books I wanted. They were by Benchley and the others, and my mother used to go into the department stores with the list in her hand. She would say, "She wants this. I don't know why. The kid's a little strange." She felt she had to apologize.

Sue Levy

Erma Bombeck: All I do is watch the human condition and write it down. It's like stealing.

We were not a well-read family. My dad was a laborer, and my mother had a fourth-grade education. I come from a whole line of laborers and Ohio farmers—people who used to wander around and find out where the crops were coming up. They would work those farms for a while and then go on to the next ones.

The person who most influenced me was my mother. She is one of the gutsiest ladies you'll ever find. My father died when she was twenty-five years old. She was left with a child—I was nine—and this child got a college education and went on to do what she always wanted to do. After my father died, my mother got a job in a factory. She was a "stator winder," but I never really knew what she did. I never knew what a stator was. She worked there for a couple of years and then got a job in a department store. In her later years she went back and worked in a factory again.

A high school English teacher, Jim Harris, encouraged me tremendously. He laughed at my humor, and he dogged me about my education. High school was going to be my cut-off point. It was the cut-off point for most girls who had to go out and get a job. That's what it was all about, and then you paid your rent at home. You paid your ten or fifteen dollars a week because your parents had raised you and now it was put-in time for you. To buy four extra years of living at home was asking too much, but Jim Harris wouldn't let go. It was great to have someone who had that much faith in me. He and his wife had no children, and they wanted to pay for my college education. My mother said, "That's ridiculous. We can afford our own. Go out and get a job." I love that.

During my four years of high school I wrote a humor column for the school paper. At sixteen I also got a job as a copy girl on the Dayton *Journal-Herald* and wound up in and out of there through the 1960s. It was a funny thing. I'm somewhere in almost every one of the pictures of the employees' summer picnics from about 1941 on. People used to say, "My God, you must be a midget or something. How old are you?"

In college I started at Ohio University but ran out of money after my first semester. So I came back and lived with my mother. I really had wanted to study journalism at Northwestern University, but you needed a lot of money. I did not know that. If you're blissfully stupid, you don't know how poor you are, because you look around your neighborhood and everyone is in the same boat. So you figure, "I'm normal." You really aren't, but you don't know that—which is great. I settled for the University of Dayton because it was a street-car college, but I wound up liking it a lot. I took morning classes so that I could work in the afternoon, and it worked out well. I was also writing humor for the newspaper and magazine at college.

After I got my degree I wrote obituaries for a year at the *Journal-Herald,* but I was so bad at them. I actually figured out a way to foul up obituaries. Then I went on to do the radio listings, and finally wound up in the women's department. Every once in a while I tried to inject a humorous personal story—about some domestic thing such as going on vacation—but newspapers were not very receptive to humor then. It was okay and it went, but not on a regular basis. I kept trying until finally, through no effort of my own, I got to do a regular column.

First, though, I left the *Journal-Herald* in 1949 to stay home and raise kids. I did some writing during the following years, but not much. Then in 1965 I got a call from Glenn Thompson, executive editor of the paper. If there is one person in this world who is responsible for what I have done, it's that man. He had joined the *Journal-Herald* after I left and didn't know me personally at all, but he asked, "How would you like to do a regular humor column for the editorial page?" I said, "It's awfully flattering, but I'm not sure I can pull it off."

We've always been a very close family, and the first thing I did— in true non-Steinem fashion—was to sit down and ask, "How is this going to affect everybody? Does anybody care?" We had no idea of what was going to happen, so I began the column. It was called "Our Girl in Centerville," which was the suburb in which we lived, and appeared twice a week.

Within weeks Glenn Thompson, unknown to me, wrote to *Newsday*, a daily newspaper on Long Island, New York, which had begun a feature syndicate. He asked if they would like to syndicate my column, and I wound up being the fourth or fifth writer they hired for syndication. I did nothing. I just sat there and watched it all happen. Glenn Thompson has never asked for a percentage and wouldn't accept one. He wanted nothing at all except the sheer joy of having unearthed someone. I am indebted to him. I stayed with the Newsday syndicate for five years until it merged with the Los Angeles Times syndicate. Then I switched to the Field Newspaper Syndicate. I think we hit thirty-eight newspapers the first year with Newsday, and I was absolutely amazed. I felt I had hit the top.

If someone had sat me down in 1965 and told me all that it was going to lead to, I would have said, "I can't do that. I cannot write a syndicated column. I cannot write books. I cannot appear on television. I cannot get up in front of thousands of people and give a speech. I can do none of that."

As a kid you don't kneel at your bedside and pray, "And please, God, when I grow up make me a syndicated columnist with 630 newspapers." At best you just hope you will fall into something. When I was growing up, I was the shyest of all my friends. Very, very shy. Very insecure. For all the usual reasons. I wasn't the prettiest girl in the room, not the most athletic, and certainly not the brightest. So you take all those things away, and what do you have? You have a very shy person. Maybe that's where the humor comes from. I think humor always is a cover-up. It's a cover-up for inadequacies. It's a cover-up for embarrassment. It's a cover-up for anything you can think of. Humor to me had been the old matter of laughing at yourself before anyone else did. That was part of what I liked from the beginning about writing. It was a private thing I could do. I could just send it out and see what it did. If someone laughed, I could stand up and say, "I did that." If they didn't laugh, nobody really cared.

There is more humor in the world than people think, but there are many different ways to approach it. I think one of the most important factors of good writing is not the mechanics—how it's put down or anything like that—but the writer's philosophy: what kind of humor is it going to be. Is it going to be cutting, biting, gentle, sarcastic, low key, personal? It's up to the individual to choose what's comfortable. I don't think anyone can teach you to write. They can put before you all kinds of literature and say, "This is how it was done" or "This is how it was done well." That's about all you can go by. You have to do your own dissecting of it. You have to figure out in your own mind why it's good—what makes it endurable, strong—if it's humor, what makes it funny. I don't think anyone in this world can teach good writing beyond providing you with good rules of grammar.

I try to make my humor gentle so that it doesn't hurt anyone. I don't like to make fun of anyone but myself, although it doesn't always work out that way. I can't stick with domesticity all the time, because people would be bored to death. So every once in a while I go beyond that domain and pick on something else. When I do— when I write a serious column on something I feel strongly about—I am bound to touch on the sensitivities of some readers. There are some people who do not have a sense of humor about themselves. It's difficult for them to laugh at themselves. That's hard for me to understand, but it does exist. I have strong feelings about not hurting people. It really bothers me, and I've got to learn to cope with it.

Once when I was autographing books in a department store, a woman practically in tears explained she was upset because her child was going to get married. The kid was twenty-four years old, and I thought, "My gosh, lady, you've done it all. You can't do anymore. You're finished with raising the child, and you don't know it." I did a column on that—on how do you regard your kids, as an investment or an insurance policy? To me they are like kites. You keep letting out the string a little bit at a time. If they soar to earth, you give a tug, watch them, and when you're sure they're up you let them go. Then just be there to kind of watch them soar. A lot of parents don't. They hang on.

Humor really depends on people's thresholds of pain and how

much they can take. For instance, a child who's sitting in a car on a vacation trip and kicking the back of the seat for 400 miles or chanting for another 250 miles, "He's looking at me again. Make him stop." About 110 percent of what I write is from such real experiences. The part I add makes us sound more clever than we really are. I put wonderful dialogue in our mouths, and we come off a lot better than we are. But the funny parts? They're pretty much the way they happen. All I do is watch the human condition and write it down. It's like stealing. I've never been too far afield from what I'm doing now. It's pretty much the same formula. It's incredible.

There are some things, of course, which just will not work. When I roll the paper into the typewriter, I feel they should, but when nothing happens I can get snow blindness from staring at the sheet. I've worked on some pieces for two days, and finally I look in the mirror and say, "Why don't you face up to the fact that it's not going to work?" Then I get hysterical, cry a little, and say, "You're absolutely right. Throw the thing away." That's when I'll do anything, if my deadline allows it, to avoid the typewriter. I make necklaces out of paper clips. Sometimes they reach down to my knees, like Bea Lillie's. I alphabetize my bills. I call up people my husband knew in the Army. I make out Christmas card lists in July. I cook. I even clean my oven. That's the absolute last straw, but I have been known to do it. Other times I can really get whipped up to write when I have something else to do. That's a crime, because those moments are so rare.

You can become very resentful of a regular column, because it begins to own you. I sometimes think the Thesaurus owns me. It seems to sit on the shelf and say, "Erma, do you want to come and play?" Yet there's never been anything else I'd rather do. I never wanted to turn into a sitting-around-the-pool, painting-my-toenails kind of person who spends hours on the telephone talking to everybody. I have a horror of that. I never was that. When I made a telephone call, it was necessary. I hate the idea of wasting time. I'm almost paranoid about it. I refuse to waste a minute. Time's too short. Life's too precious. I don't know why I'm so driven. There's no need for it, except that I'm so geared up and used to filling every minute.

My first book was a collection of columns. I had been with Newsday two years when they asked me to do it. It started out in 1967 as a real sleeper. It didn't sell particularly well, but they kept it in print. Then as the readership of the column grew, that little book grew and grew and grew, and it's still selling.

My baptism of fire on television was the *Tonight Show* with Johnny Carson. It was when the first book came out and we were kicking it off. I was sitting in the hotel room in New York with my mother and thinking, "I can't do this. I'm too introverted." Just before it was time to leave for the studio, I said to my mom, "I think I'm going to spit up. I don't see how I possibly can get through this night. There's no way." My mother said, "You're probably right, if you think you can pretend you're something you're not. But if you just go out there, be honest, and do the best you can, I know you can do it." That's how I got through the night, and I'll never forget that.

Everything really has been a spin-off. The column begat the books. The books begat the television. The television begat the lectures. Each time, I said to myself, "I can't do that," but I gave it my best shot. The regular appearances on *Good Morning, America* came about in 1975 when the American Broadcasting Company was putting together a magazine format for the show. For ten years I had resisted television offers and told my agent that what I really wanted was a Benchley-type format where I could lay it out a little and make fun of myself. When Bob Shanks of ABC came out to Phoenix from New York, I said, "Gee, I don't know. I don't think I want to do that." My agent then reminded me that that was exactly what I had wanted. So we taped a month's shows, and it went.

There are facets you really don't know you have unless you try them. That's the fun part of it. I'm learning. I'm learning a lot because every type of writing is different. With *Good Morning,*

America I had to get used to the spoken word, and that's a whole different thing from the written word.

It's hard to compare your present situation with something else when you don't know what might have been, but this all has given me a confidence I never expected to have. To come from schoolgirl shyness to a point where I can deliver a talk to four thousand people—or even to where I can look people in the eye, extend my hand, and say hello—is a monumental step for me. I probably would have become a recluse housewife picking lint off the refrigerator or something. I don't know. This has opened a whole new world for me. I have found out things about myself—things I can do that I never dreamed I could do.

David Brenner

COMEDIAN

Coming off the ghetto streets of Philadelphia, David Brenner followed the routine pattern of street kids— spending two years in military service after high school. An encounter with an Army buddy in Germany, however, encouraged him to enter college, and he graduated with high honors from Temple University, where he majored in mass communications. This eventually led to a brief career at various television stations as a writer/ producer/director of documentaries, for which he received a number of awards, including a regional Emmy. Then, with that career soaring, he quit to try his luck as a stand-up comedian. He achieved just minor success in the field until, after a year, he auditioned and won a guest spot on the Tonight Show. *In 1977 the American Guild of Variety Artists saluted him as the nation's leading comedian—chosen by the vote of his fellow performers—and on network television presented him with the Male Comedy Star of the Year Award.*

As a kid growing up in a city ghetto it seemed that once you had two numbers in your age you were unhappy. Something seemed to happen when you got that other number, because everybody growing up was so damned unhappy. If you were eight or seven you still had a shot. So I started lying about my age when I was nine. I just wanted to stay a kid.

I went through the normal fantasies of wanting to be a big gunfighter in the Wild West or a great boxer, a world-champion boxer. I fantasized about those things, but I never had a career idea in my head—not once. I never had a direction except to get away from being poor. Once you found out that not everybody was in the pits, you figured, "Hey, I want to get out." It was so rank to live that way, so goddamn bad, that it pushed you to get out. A lot went out the wrong way or didn't get out. But I always had a positive attitude, and you have to have a positive attitude to get out; you can't do it with negativism. You just can't, because then life will beat you.

My mother was in her mid-forties—in the midst of all the poverty with two children and my father unemployed—when she discovered she was pregnant with me. My parents didn't tell me until a few years ago, but they tried in every way to abort me. After the procedure, the doctor told my mom, "I don't know what's in there, whether it's a boy or a girl baby, but medically it should be dead, and it's alive. I've never seen a life force like that in all the years I've been delivering babies. I think it's supposed to do something in life. You ought to give it the chance to do it." That's when she decided to carry me. She just figured, "Well, we'll split the milk bottle five ways instead of four."

My father probably was the strongest influence in my life. He had been a vaudeville comedian—a song and dance man. He performed from the time he was nine until he was twenty-one, and he quit before he married my mother. He's still the funniest man in the world, brilliantly funny, but he gave up show business for security,

David Brenner: *I've found that the difference between a niche and a rut sometimes can't be distinguished; you think you've found your niche, and you don't realize you're in a rut.*

and we never had it. We just lived insecure all our lives. He tried to discourage me from going into show business because of the insecurity, but, at the same time, he would spin dreams of what it was like being on stage and making people laugh. He had us laughing all the time, because, if you make fun of what hurts, it takes away some of the sting.

Laughter's not a medicine that's going to cure anything, but it is a salve that softens the pain. We had a sofa that was one of the damndest things I ever saw. There were two springs that would shoot out of it on their own volition. One shot out from the bottom. You would hear this noise as it broke loose from the board and shot into the floor. We had to pull it loose from the floor and the rug and force it back into place. The other one came through the cushion. Suddenly it would pop through the cushion and, *boing*, this spring would be sticking up there. If it happened when company was at the house, my father would say something like, "You can put your hat on it if you want," as if it were some kind of device. Or he would say, "We put apples on that. Do you want an apple to put on it?" The jokes eased the tension—the embarrassment of being poor and not able to buy a sofa—and the laughter just kept us all from crying. So we made fun of everything. There were great laughs in our house, great roaring and screaming.

If it hadn't been for that, I'd probably be in jail now like a lot of guys—if I were alive; if I didn't get onto drugs and die from an overdose. My whole personality was inflammatory, spontaneous, irrational at times. In the house I was a good kid because my parents were too old to take anything from me. My mother would say, "I'm going to take a nap. Don't make any noise." And I wouldn't. If a teacher told me, "Don't make any noise," I'd throw a chair through the window. I had no discipline outside. I would have gone overboard were it not for my father's sense of humor, the love at home, and the closeness of my friends on the street.

The guys on the corner were the greatest influence on my life after my father. We were so closely knit it was as though we were all from the same parents. Everybody was a brother, and that allegiance exists to this day. We still have deals based on a handshake. You would never say to anyone, "Okay, we'll do that. Yeah. I'll do that for you," and then shake hands and not do it. That would never happen. They might go into a grocery store and beat up someone, but they would never break a deal. It's a very strange code of ethics on the street, but there's also greatness to it. I used to think, "Oh, to get out of the street and into the honest, clean world." The only difference—and this is to the credit of the street—is that, if someone didn't like you on the street and was going to get you, he told you right up front, "The next time I see you, I'm going to kick your ass." Whereas in the nice world that I've moved into, they smile and shake your hand and then go and do something behind your back. There was none of that on the street. It was all up front, one on one.

The guys on the corner also were an outlet for my sense of humor. They helped me mold it by laughing and encouraging me in the rough ways we had—"Come on, Brenner. Hey, go ahead, Brenner." So I would do or say things, and while I was doing them they would be laughing. That really encouraged me. It helped refine the sense of humor my father had given me.

The street also gives you status even though you have nothing. My friends on the street gave me a sense of being. I was a leader among them, and I belonged. A lot of people talk about comedians seeking love and belonging. I had all that. Great love in my house and great love with my friends. I was president of my class from fourth grade through twelfth. I was the most popular kid in the school and popular with the girls. I dated the prettiest girl in the class all the time. I had all that. It was the positive side of the street that gave it to me, and it gave me a pride in myself.

We lived in two neighborhoods in Philadelphia. The first was South Philadelphia, and from the south end we moved to the west end. West Philadelphia, when we first moved there, was a Jewish ghetto with black, Italian, Irish, and mixed Armenian-Greek neighborhoods surrounding it. We actually were on the periphery of the

Jewish neighborhood, one of two Jewish families on our street. When the black neighborhood started moving into the Jewish neighborhood, the Jewish neighborhood started moving out. Soon the Brenners were the only white family left, and we stayed for twelve years as the only white family in the neighborhood. My father may have been poor and he may have been unsuccessful in the eyes of the world, but he is a principled man. He always said no one should run from another human being unless the other person is no good. Not only did he say it, he lived it. So we lived there, and I don't think I had another street fight once the neighborhood turned black.

After high school I kicked around the streets for a while before going into the service. I had scored highly on some Army aptitude tests and was put into cryptography—code work. There were twelve of us in our unit in Germany, and I was the only non-college one. I associated with two crowds. There was the street crowd, the guys from the rough city environment I was used to. The other crowd was the college graduates. All of a sudden I was playing both sides of the fence. I enjoyed both sides and have stayed straddling that fence to this day.

The college guys used to discuss and debate. One of them was John Kearney—from Wilkes-Barre, Pennsylvania—and one day I put him down real bad. I creamed him verbally, and he said, "Brenner, you know why you joke around so much?" I thought, "Oh, he's going to open himself up for another slam," and I said, "No. Tell me why, John." He said, "Because you have nothing intelligent to say." I came back with a few lines, and everybody laughed, but I was boiling mad. Then I started thinking, "Why am I angry? Come on, it wasn't that important." And I realized he was right. He had hit a nerve ending and had cut me to the quick. I really didn't know what to say about a lot of subjects, and that was why I joked around—just as I had used joking to deal with the environment I had grown up in.

A few days later he came in when I was on late duty and said, "I couldn't get all the information. You have to fill in some of the places." He laid down a college application. He had gone to head-quarters and gotten information such as my parents' names and all else that was in my records, but there were certain areas he didn't have. He said, "You have to fill these in, and when you do you get your ass in college, because that's where you belong," and he walked out.

I thought, "What a wise guy." Then I looked the application over and started thinking about what he had said to me earlier. I filled it out, applied for a scholarship, and got into Temple University in Philadelphia. I majored in mass communications—radio, television, and journalism—because I always had been interested in writing and wanted to do something creative. I also wanted to express myself and express ideas and be in touch with people. Actually I had been thinking about television drama, but it was a dying thing then. When I graduated from Temple, it was with high honors.

I sent out close to five hundred letters with my résumé attached. I wrote to every television station in the country. Then I gave up on TV and went for federal jobs. I sat there in that damned apartment—day after day and night after night—typing letters. I was living in a ghetto apartment in the same neighborhood with the damn silverfish, those damn bugs, scooting all around. Sweaty and with no air conditioning. Finally from all those letters I got one job offer—as a customs guard in San Francisco. I figured, "What the hell did I go to school for? I spent all those hours studying, and I don't believe this." Looking back now, I wish I had gone to college just for a year and quit. I had worked since I was in the ninth grade—in a supermarket butcher shop, in a Christmas ornament factory, in an ice cream plant loading the trucks and bicycles. Now I couldn't get a job, and I didn't want to go back to hustling on the street.

One night I was sitting in the apartment watching my beat-up television set, and Rod Serling came on and did a commercial. I wrote to him: "How can you, a great writer, do a commercial? What are you selling products for? You have really disappointed me." He answered, and he explained the realities of the business—that the commercials enabled him to do his writing. That sometimes you have to do it. But he also told me, "Stay on, because it's guys like you who believe what you believe that can help this industry. Don't give up." That letter kept a spark alive, just one little spark, and I figured, "Why not fight on?" Years later I had a chance to thank him. I was flying out to California to do the *Tonight Show*, and he was on the plane.

During that summer, Bill Seibel, who had been one of my professors at Temple, called on a Friday afternoon to tell me about a job opening at NBC in Philadelphia. It was for about eleven or thirteen weeks' work as a documentary writer. I sat down right away and started to write an outline for a documentary—"A Neighborhood in Transition." It was the subject I knew best, about a white neighborhood becoming black. I stayed up straight through Monday morning, writing and meeting with Bill. He would say, "No, change this around. Go back and do that over."

Monday morning, sleepless since Friday, I went in for the interview. The guy asked me, "What do you know about writing for film?" I said, "Nothing." He asked me, "What do you know about directing?" I said, "Nothing." He asked me, "What do you know about editing film?" I said, "Look, that's the third question you've asked me, and the answer still is 'Nothing,' and probably for every question you ask me the answer is going to be 'Nothing,' because I know nothing. If you're after experience, I'm not your man. Bring in someone from New York, someone established. But if you're after potential, no one is going to work harder or faster than I am. I'm the best in potential; I'm the worst in experience. So your decision is whether you're going to go with experience or potential. Here's my writing. Read what I did." Then I got up and said, "I'm sorry. I'm taking up your time, and I'm embarrassing myself."

I went home and called Bill. "I don't believe what I just did," I told him. "I was in there for about four minutes at the most, and I blew it." He asked, "What did you do?" I said, "I don't want to talk about it. I'm going to go to sleep. I'm sorry I let you down."

Two days later I got a call from the guy at NBC. He said, "Come in tomorrow at nine." I figured, "I can't take the embarrassment of another interview," but I said, "I'll tell you what. I got a few things to do"—which I did—"could we make it in the afternoon?" He said, "Well, the studio opens at nine." I said, "I appreciate that, but I really do have a few things to do. Could I come in for the interview in the afternoon?" He said, "I don't think you understand. You've got the job. You start working at nine." "I'll see you at nine," I told him.

That day, the day I landed the job, I was down to eighty cents. It was on the dresser, and after the telephone call I picked it up and wrapped it in a rag. Then I went out and borrowed $20 on the street and celebrated. I told myself that someday I would put those three quarters and nickel on a black velvet background along with a little plaque saying "Lest we forget" and put a sterling silver frame around it. "Someday I'll have a den," I thought, "and I'll put that in front of me so that, if I ever think I'm a big deal, I can look at it and see the eighty cents." I have it there now because I promised myself I would do it, but I don't look at it anymore. I don't need it. I've got that eighty cents in my head.

After that I bounced to a few stations. CBS in Chicago. Back to Philadelphia, where I headed up documentary production for Westinghouse Broadcasting. On to New York, where I did some things for Metromedia. Then into Public Broadcasting. I changed jobs fast because I learned that, if you don't, people ask, "Why isn't he moving?" So I moved—up, up, up—until I got a $30,000 job offer in 1969. It seemed like the apex of my career, a job going around the world doing featurettes for network television. It was what I had imagined I would most want to do, but something was missing; something was wrong.

I went away to the islands—the West Indies. I had a little, inexpensive cottage and was going to the beach every day. Then it started to rain. Three straight days of rain, and I listened to the radio and I was thinking, "What am I doing? I've got this great job offer with a *carte blanche* expense account. What am I doing on an island thinking about it?" But I also was listening to the news on the radio. It was so depressing—all the reports about everything that was wrong in the world. I thought to myself, "Why don't people laugh? If you don't laugh, you'll never get through the day with that news." So then I thought, "What the hell. Why am I trying to make a decision now? Let me be a comedian for a year. I've got $9,000 in the bank. I'll go back to the way I used to live."

I came back to New York, and I called up the guy. I said, "Thank you very much for the offer, but I can't take it." He said, "Let's negotiate. Does someone else want you? Is it the money? Is it this? Is it that?" I said, "It's a sensational job, a job I've always wanted. I'm quitting television." He asked, "What are you going to do?" and I told him, "I want to be a stand-up comedian." He cracked up, and I said, "Thanks for my first laugh."

I went one year as I said I would, performing almost every night in spots around the New York area. The Improvisation on West 44th Street, which was a freebie, Pips Coffee House in Sheepshead Bay for $30 a weekend, a lot of clubs in Greenwich Village, and other places all over town—little clubs, nothing bars, joints. There was a clique of us, all street guys trying to get our careers started. Once again it was back to the streets. Hanging out on the corner. Shooting pool late at night. I got back to the old things—the camaraderie, everyone struggling to make something of himself. I was back in the fight again. It was invigorating.

I've found that the difference between a niche and a rut sometimes can't be distinguished; you think you've found your niche, and you don't realize you're in a rut. My mother used to say, "David, do what you want to do. Do what makes you happy. Don't live a life you don't like. Try to be happy." I would rather fail a hundred times before I would fail to try something. There's nothing wrong with failure. Nothing. Try twenty careers, fifty careers. Try to change your job. Try to change your luck. When you fail to try, that's failure—giving up; not trying.

At the end of that year, I had just about run out of money. The $9,000 was gone, plus what I had earned as a comedian. So I thought, "I should try for the *Tonight Show*," and I did. Right before Christmas 1970, I auditioned at the J. Victor Theater near Rockefeller Plaza. On January 7, Rick Bernstein, my agent then and my personal manager now, called me. "You're on the *Tonight Show* tomorrow night," he said. I got together with my creative consultant, George Schultz, the owner of Pips Coffee House in Brooklyn and the first person to believe in me. We went over what I was going to do, and on January 8, I went on the *Tonight Show*, which was still out of New York then. The audience reaction was great—a fantasy come true. That time I was down to just $3, which isn't in a frame. I figured the eighty cents was enough. Within two days I had $10,000 worth of job offers. So this lark, this hiatus, this interim period of comedy, turned into a career.

Then about 1975 I hit a low spot. I was a very good opening-act comedian for a lot of big names, and I was doing okay on the talk shows. The *Tonight Show* always was behind me. So were Mike Douglas and Merv Griffin—and David Frost when he had his show. But the rest of the industry was cold on me. The word was out that Brenner had had his shot and it was over with. You couldn't get me on a variety show. Situation comedy? Ice cold. Las Vegas? Ice cold. The big clubs? They booked me only if I was with a big name. I think it was because they didn't understand my sense of humor, and, because they didn't, they assumed the public didn't. But my father always had told me, "Never listen to a man with a briefcase. Listen to the people. The people tell you what they are thinking."

So I told Rick Bernstein, "Rick, I see the fan mail. I see the reaction on the streets when I walk down them. I can't go into a restaurant and eat, because of the people. I can't go shopping, because of the people. You can't tell me that I'm not hot just because the industry says I'm not hot. I think I am hot and that I can get red hot if we go to the people—just like a politician talking in every little town from the back of a train. You've got to get me to the people. Get me into any rooms for any money. I don't care what the money is. I'll do heavy television, plug the dates, and go to the rooms. Let's see how we do. I'll give it one year, because I'm going to quit. I'm not going to be a journeyman comedian. That's not my idea of success."

That year I did 104 network appearances. The year before, I had done 36. I did something like 10 Carsons, 20 Griffins, 25 Douglases. On and on. I hit that tube, and there wasn't a week I wasn't on it. In addition, I started to headline. We went to one club, and we asked for $5,000 for the week. They said, "No. What does Brenner mean? He's good on television. We like him. But we won't give him that kind of money." I told Rick, "Forget about the money. Tell them I want two dollars a person—three on weekends." At the end of the week, the guy signed a check for over $26,000. I called Rick in California. I said, "Take out a pencil and paper and write this down: Three thousand . . . nine hundred . . . twenty-four dollars . . . and fifteen cents." He asked, "Is that what you made?" I said, "No. That's what you made. That's your 15 percent, my man." He went crazy. I said, "Start booking me." And then we started. Everyplace we went, we broke the house record. All the big names, all the big names in the business, I was busting their records. Biggest attendance in ten years. Biggest attendance in eight years. Biggest crowd ever. Then we started putting it in the trade papers.

As I thought, I wasn't cold. The industry had been cold on me. It culminated—that stage of my career—in Philadelphia in September 1976. Every weekend that summer they had a different celebrity do a free concert at the Philadelphia Museum of Art to commemorate the Bicentennial. A close friend of mine who had his own television show had drawn 17,000 people. I figured, "It's my hometown. I should do 20,000–22,000." Then, on my way there, it suddenly dawned on me that it was Labor Day weekend. On Labor Day weekend in Philadelphia you can steal the houses and not get caught, because everyone is either at the shore, in the park, picnicking, or somewhere out of the city. I thought, "Oh, God, Labor Day weekend! I'm going to be embarrassed. Please let me do just the

17,000, or at least 15,000. Then I can always say it was Labor Day weekend."

The streets from the airport to the hotel were empty. There was hardly a soul in the center city. I panicked. I figured, "This is it. I'm going to be ruined. I'll be lucky to draw 8,000." Normally that's nice, but not when everyone else is drawing 12,000, 15,000, 17,000. They drove me in in a van, and I couldn't see. I asked the policeman inside, "How is it out there?" He said, "We stopped counting an hour ago." I said, "What do you mean?" He said, "We stopped counting when we estimated 46,000." It turned out to be the record for the season.

I'm lucky to be able to have an idea pop into my head, to be able to spill it out on the stage, and to make people—strangers—laugh. That's an acceptance of one's creativity. There's both a selfish and an altruistic side to all of this. The selfish is that I have to get paid for it. The altruistic is that I know what humor did for me in easing my life. I know how much it meant for me —whether it came from me, my father, or some of my funny friends—and now I'm lucky to be able to give it to other people for five minutes a night on television or forty-five minutes in a club. That's very rewarding.

The most rewarding part of it—and this is all personal—is that I have put an end in the Brenner family to four hundred years of poverty. It stops here! Here and now it stops! The Brenners will no longer be poor! It's selfish, but that's it. It stops here!

Yvonne Brathwaite Burke

CONGRESSWOMAN

U.S. Representative Yvonne Brathwaite Burke, Democrat from California, is a native of Los Angeles. A graduate of the University of Southern California law school, she was a practicing attorney and active community leader for ten years before her election to the California state legislature in 1966. She was elected to Congress in 1972, and at the 1968, 1972, and 1976 Democratic National Conventions she was active in drafting her party's platform. She was the first woman elected to Congress from California in more than twenty years and the first black woman ever elected to the House from her state. Among the many citations she has received for her governmental and civic activities, she was designated in 1974 by Time *magazine as one of America's two hundred future leaders.*

Early experiences carry over. I grew up in situations where, as a child from a ghetto, the odds always were against me. I was an only ·child without brothers or sisters to protect me, so I had to fight by myself, and I think that is why I am as aggressive as I am in never accepting things as they are but fighting back. I fought from my earliest years, and it terrified my parents. They were not people who agreed with that kind of approach. My dad used to meet me as often as he could at school to protect me from any trouble on my way home.

My parents came to California in the early 1920s from Paris, Texas, where my mother taught school and my father was a farmer. They left because the atmosphere was very bad there for blacks. It was a time when there were a lot of lynchings, and my father was in great danger. He had gotten into a disagreement of some sort with the man who owned the general store. As a result, there were threats made against him. So my parents decided to leave rather than take a chance on my father being lynched. They went first to Arizona, but they stayed there just a short while before going to California. My mother worked as a maid in a restroom in a Los Angeles department store until she began working in real estate in the 1940s, and my father got a job as a janitor at the Metro-Goldwyn-Mayer movie studios.

The first elementary school I attended was in the East Los Angeles ghetto where we lived, but the principal determined—because of my abilities, I guess—that I should go to another school where I could get a better education. So in the fourth grade I began taking the bus to the 32nd Street elementary school. It was a training school for education majors at the University of Southern California. I was the only black child at the school, and the attitude of the other children toward me was totally antagonistic. They called me every name in the book. If I had an apple with me for lunch, they tried to take it away. In the schoolyard they would push me away from the

Yvonne Brathwaite Burke: All people probably have a lot of things they would have done differently, but I have very positive feelings about the things I went through. Many of them hurt at the time, but there are few things that hurt or bother me today. I'm past that.

monkey bars and other equipment. But I fought back. Boys never intimidated me, and I never felt I had to run from them. I took lessons on the violin in those years. So I always had it with me, and I would swing my violin case at anyone I had trouble with on the way home from school.

There are some negative aftereffects from having gone through all the indignities and all the name-calling and other things—both during the early and later years—but I have no hatred or bitterness. The end result mostly is positive in terms of the traits those experiences helped me develop. For one thing, they helped me learn that people can win when the odds are against them. I think that, unless people are basically hard, they have to have endured early difficulties in order to be able to fight some of the battles in later life.

In a city like Los Angeles I had to sue many, many people. I sued because I was refused admittance to a dance studio, and in Sacramento I had to sue in order to get an apartment to live in. I walked on my first picket line when I was fourteen. My father helped to organize the Building Services Union at M-G-M, and the picketing was an attempt to get the actors to support the strike. I was very much a part of that labor fight.

I read a great deal as a child. I suppose it was partly a retreat from the prejudices to which I was exposed, but it helped me with vocabulary and in formulating ideas when, during high school, I became deeply interested in public speaking and debate. I spent most of my free time developing my ability as a debater. I practiced every afternoon, the same way you would practice for competition in sports. I was a member of the debating team, and my speech teacher—Mr. Stengel—coached me all through high school. He was very helpful. I entered a lot of debate competitions and earned a number of scholarships as a result of them.

In college I became active in drama and had some passing thoughts about becoming an actress, but my most serious thoughts were of law, which is why I majored in political science. As a student in high school, I had gone to a birthday party at the home of Loren

Miller for his nephew, who was a friend of mine. Loren Miller, a constitutional lawyer, was a great hero of us all. He had won a case in 1948, *Stanley vs. Kremer,* which set aside the restrictive covenants on land that forced all blacks to live in small areas in Los Angeles, and it greatly improved the conditions under which we lived in the city. Those covenants, which the case proved unconstitutional, restricted anyone but Caucasians from purchasing certain residential properties. I never had met Loren Miller until that party, and when I saw him in his study surrounded by his books I think I really decided at that moment that I wanted to go to law school. It's an experience I share. His nephew became a lawyer and his son is a judge, and they both were at the party.

I had a scholarship to the University of California. I started at the Berkeley campus, but after a year and a half I transferred to the Los Angeles campus. There was not much of a social life at Berkeley for a black girl because it was almost totally a white environment, but I also wanted to save as much money as I could for law school. So I went to UCLA and lived at home.

When I graduated from college I enrolled at the University of Southern California because its law school was the most prestigious of any in southern California. That was during the early years of the civil rights movement, and I became very much involved in it. I worked part-time for the NAACP and devoted to it all of my time outside of law school and my studies. I graduated from law school in 1956, passed my bar examination that December, and went into private practice. There weren't many alternatives available to me as a black woman. Hardly any private law firms hired women in those days, and there were very, very few jobs available to blacks in government. It took major changes for that to come about, and even when I took a civil service job as a deputy corporation commissioner, the manager told me, "Any waves and we'll put a black mark on your civil service record." He knew I had been active in any number of civic, community, and political organizations and that I continually had fought to correct inequities I saw in the system.

It wasn't until I began to practice law that I fully realized how incapable poor people are of dealing with the system. Many of those who came to my office needed help with such things as answering letters, dealing with credit problems, and the like. A key turning point for me was the Watts riots in August 1965, when I was working as a hearing officer for the Police Commission. I used the parking lot at the police headquarters for my car, and I was going down to it on the first day of the riots when I saw the officers running and yelling. It was almost a carnival atmosphere. I went back to my office to try to find out what was happening. As soon as I learned of the riots in Watts, Florence Vaughan, who was a real estate broker with an office on the same floor as mine, and I drove into the heart of the community. It was a terrifying thing, but I felt I had to do it.

I had never seen anything like what I saw that day, and it stupefied me. It was total chaos, and I was in complete shock. Burning and looting were going on all around us. People were running every which way, and the police were arresting people by the hundreds. It was obvious there would be a tremendous need for a legal defense mechanism to assist the people being arrested—an emergency system to help them get in touch with attorneys, to let wives find husbands and parents find children. So with the help of some friends, I set up that mechanism through the NAACP while the riots still were going on. Afterwards, the attorneys of the McCone Commission, which investigated the riots, sought me out to work on their staff.

Many of us who worked on that commission report recognized that there was a great need for change in the political leadership, for new dimensions of leadership, younger leadership. We started looking at the figures. We learned that the numbers of minorities in some of the ghetto districts were under-misrepresented. As a result, there were not sufficient support services for all the needs of the poor, and they also were not properly represented in government. We made a lot of projections based on our findings and recognized that major changes were necessary to prevent a recurrence of the riots—and that the solutions, at least in part, involved legislation. When we learned that the state legislator from my district was not planning to run for re-election, Sam Williams, the chief attorney on the McCone Commission's legal staff, talked me into running for the legislature. He became my campaign manager, and in 1966 I was elected to represent the Sixty-third District in the California state assembly.

Gus Hawkins, a congressman from the neighboring district, was an important person in that campaign. I had first met him when he came to lecture at UCLA while I was a student there. He was one of the few politicians I got to know before I went into politics myself. He was very supportive—never discouraging—and he assisted me in many ways. George Hardy, the international president of my father's union, also was interested in the idea of my running and eventually voted to support me. That was a major endorsement, because the support of organized labor was very important in the district. The union's executive committee actually had voted to back another candidate in the primary, but we managed to throw it into a floor fight at a meeting of the representatives of the union locals from throughout Los Angeles County and upset the executive committee's recommendations. I have never been part of a political machine. No one has ever just handed me a district.

There were many reasons why I finally won in the November election. I was well known in the community, and I think the fact that I was a woman helped. At the time, the district was only about thirty percent black—I've never represented a district where the majority was black—but the people understood the issues I identified with and recognized those issues as being more important than anything else.

I really thought, in that first election, that I was going into politics part time, which is what the state legislature usually involves since it is in session only a certain portion of the year, allowing the legislators to pursue their private professions. In 1966, the year I was elected, the California constitution was changed, and the legislature became full time. If I had known I was going to wind up in national politics, I'm not sure I would have gotten involved in the first place, but I certainly don't regret it.

I have very few regrets. All people probably have a lot of things they would have done differently, but I have very positive feelings about the things I went through. Many of them hurt at the time, but there are few things that hurt or bother me today. I'm past that. I know I can win, just as I knew that the things I believed in ultimately would win. It's all just a matter of time and effort and sometimes a lot of defeats.

Mary S. Calderone

HUMAN DEVELOPMENT PIONEER

Dr. Mary S. Calderone is president of SIECUS, *the Sex Information and Education Council of the United States, of which she was a co-founder in 1964. Prior to that she was medical director of the Planned Parenthood Federation of America for eleven years. Born in New York City in 1904, the daughter of the distinguished photographer Edward Steichen, she spent her early years in France. She is a graduate of Vassar College, the University of Rochester medical school, and the Columbia University School of Public Health. In 1971, the* Ladies Home Journal *cited her as one of the seventy-five most important women in America. The* Newspaper Enterprise Association *listed her as one of the fifty most influential women in America in 1975.*

I was a late starter. It took me an extra long time to find out what I really wanted to do. The only personal ambition I recollect ever having was to do something worthwhile no matter what it was.

I always was dissatisfied with the way I was. I knew that I was very selfish, very hardheaded, very stubborn. I wasn't loved very much by my peers. In school I was admired a lot, maybe envied, but I wasn't loved, and I wanted to be somebody other people would love. It took me a long time to come to terms with that. As long as I was self-conscious and being the glamorous young woman who spoke French perfectly, who attended Vassar, who could ride horses better than anybody else, as long as I was that person, there wasn't any reason for me to get close to other people and learn how to love them, which is the first step in being loved. I had to have some tough experiences before I knuckled under.

The death of my mentor, Mrs. George Pratt, was a great sorrow. Helen Sherman Pratt was a wonderful woman. She was a dear friend and patron of my father. She took me, the daughter of a poor young artist, under her wing. She paid for the music lessons when I took up the piano, and she provided the money which sent me to college. She had an incredible quality of letting me know that she believed in me even when telling me she wished I would behave differently. She had confidence in me, yet she was discriminating about it, holding out ideals to me. She died during my early years at Vassar. That was a great sorrow and loss.

Then some years later my oldest daughter's death from pneumonia at the age of ten was unspeakable. I knew I had to live through that; get on top of it. But I was in the egotistical framework of "Why did this happen to me?" "Why this child?" "Why my child?" This just fed into my sorrow and my bitterness and my anger that it should have happened. Then one morning I suddenly woke up and realized that my hands were reaching out to many, many mothers before me and after me; that I was just one in a long, long chain of

Mary S. Calderone: *The people who most influenced my life . . . all shared one common trait: the unique ability to discipline me emotionally and intellectually while at the same time conveying their love and total belief that I could and eventually would live up to their expectations.*

mothers who had lost or who would lose their loved children. This put the whole thing in perspective for me. The reality of that began to help me find my balance.

From the beginning I knew that my father loved me. I had many conflicts with my mother, and my parents were divorced when I was fourteen. Before that, though, when I was about eighteen months old, my parents brought me to France. We lived there until I was ten, and it had a great effect on my life. My father was part of a group of artist friends at the turn of the century that included Rodin, Matisse, and Brancusi. It was an atmosphere of passionate appreciation of beauty and a passionate disregard for forms and formality that had its influence on me as a child. I was highly emotional in terms of being responsive to and very much aware of the gifts of life, of feeling, of beauty, and of song. These were all around me. My father gave me that. He gave it to me by the way he saw everything—children, flowers, animals. He was joyous and full of life. He saw beauty and instantly drew it out.

It was a free growing-up. I didn't go to school until I was nine, but I was reading voraciously by then. My favorites were the books of the Andrew Lang fairy tale series, tales from many countries. I lived for them. I was fortunate during those years to experience stimulating conversation in our home when my father's friends dropped by to talk. It seems I always was exposed to good talk, both in France and then back in the United States. Later, in my teens, one of my greatest pleasures was sitting and feeling a part of the good talk of vigorous, stimulating people.

At the outbreak of the First World War we fled France and spent a dreary winter in a summer cottage in Connecticut which had been loaned to us. I went to school there, and with my French accent and independent ways my schoolmates regarded me as a very strange child. A year later I was enrolled in Brearley School in New York City and lived in the home of Dr. Leopold Stieglitz. He was the brother of Alfred Stieglitz, the noted photographer, who was a friend of my father's. Until then, art was one of my principal interests. I did a lot of paintings full of the spontaneous expression of children which we adults so often destroy. The first day at Brearley they sat me down and said, "Draw that plaster cast of a lion." That was the end. I dropped everything I ever had done with art. Right then. It was finished, killed. I realize, though, that I mustn't really have had much talent or I would have persisted anyway.

My first biology class at Brearley at the age of fourteen was different. That was when I really became hooked on science. It was the most exciting thing. The teacher, Miss Littell, anesthetized a frog, and we crowded around and watched her. She cut down its abdomen. Then she cut across and laid back the four little flaps—thin, thin skin. I didn't know what I was going to see when she cut into the abdominal cavity. I had vague visions of messiness, blood, and all around in there unmentionable things. But the beauty, the startling beauty. Orderly, beautiful organs spread before my eyes: the heart pumping, the lungs breathing, the intestines lying together so beautifully. The colors were beautiful. The way they fit together and moved against each other was just unbelievable. That was when my real excitement about science awoke.

Before puberty I had vague ideas of being a pianist. I was able to play with a depth of feeling that swept everybody off his feet, but I was awful technically because I wouldn't work at it. I had thought of being a concert pianist, but once I knew I would never excel at it I dropped it. I was interested in poetry too. My favorite poet was Vachel Lindsay. His poems were so exciting. I also liked Carl Sandburg even though I didn't understand him, because he had married my father's sister. I began to write poetry myself, but as soon as I realized I could never be a great poet I lost interest in that too. This pattern repeated itself over and over. I kept throwing myself wholeheartedly into new pursuits until the time came when I saw I couldn't be first-rate at them.

Later on when I was almost thirty, I learned from aptitude tests I took at the suggestion of my analyst that this was all part of being what the Johnson O'Connor Human Engineering Laboratory calls the "too many aptitudes person." Unless I could use all my aptitudes I would continue to wander from one thing to another. Using some and not the others produced a restlessness in me. So I'd turn around, do the opposite, and get restless again. I simply didn't find myself until I found an area where all my aptitudes, except one or two, could be used, and that didn't happen until at the age of thirty-one I went into medicine on the advice of Johnson O'Connor. (It's interesting that vocabulary is the one correlate to success Johnson O'Connor ever found. He did hundreds of thousands of aptitude testings and followed up on them. High language people, he found, have more of a chance for success no matter what they try.)

By my junior year at Brearley I had become bored with high school. I went directly to Vassar to begin my pre-medical studies, but by the end of my junior year I became restless once more. I had completed all my pre-med courses and was so sick and tired of chemistry and everything that went with it that I simply threw it all by the board and in my last year studied nothing but drama, music, and English. When I graduated I turned fully to the stage. I became thoroughly caught up in the theater and thought I had left medicine behind. Maria Ouspenskaya and Boleslavski had come to this country from the Moscow Art Theatre and got funding to establish the American Laboratory Theater. It was intended to be in this country what the Moscow Art Theatre was in Russia. I studied with them for three years, but by then I was married with one child and pregnant with another. I decided two children were reason enough to take me out of there. I wasn't as good as I wanted to be anyway.

I continued in the mode of a flashy, brilliant young woman, but I really didn't know how to give. I recognized it as a failing, but I didn't know how to get out of it so that I could make a warm, simple, giving, loving relationship. It was a wretched marriage for my husband. It was for me too, but I'm sure it was much worse for him. After our divorce in 1930 I worked in a department store to support myself and my two daughters, but I quickly learned that commerce was not my bag.

The following year I returned to medicine. I was much more ready for it at age thirty-one. My purpose was purely utilitarian. I was a divorced woman with two children, and I had to find a way to support them. But, for almost the first time in my life, I was being someone I liked. It was during my late twenties that, recognizing my failures and weaknesses, I had sought help through psychoanalysis. That was tremendously important, but my satisfaction with myself came from more than that. The people who most influenced my life—my father; Aunt Charlotte, who was my mother's sister; Mrs. Pratt; and Ann Dunn, a great teacher at Brearley who instilled in me that I must face up to myself and develop work habits—all shared one common trait: the unique ability to discipline me emotionally and intellectually while at the same time conveying their love and total belief that I could and eventually would live up to their expectations.

I was ten years older than everyone else at the University of Rochester medical school, and it was hard. But I made a deliberate effort to knuckle under, and I stayed with my studies. I graduated in 1939. Medicine gave me a solid foundation. There are so many things you can do with a medical degree. It's a passport to success, and you can do with it almost anything if you are a creative person. After a year's internship at Bellevue Hospital, I decided to go into public health. This too was pure practicality. It meant an eventual nine-to-five job, and I would be with my surviving child. I felt I could not be away from her during the years of residency that would have been required to prepare for practice. During this period while I was supported by a $2,400-a-year fellowship, I met Frank Calderone. He was a health officer at the Lower East Side Health Center and at the beginning of a distinguished medical career that was to include the New York City Health Department, the World Health Organization, and the United Nations Secretariat Health Services.

In 1941, the year I received my master's degree in public health from Columbia University, I remarried at the age of thirty-seven.

Over the following years I raised two more daughters and began working several hours a day—although I never really considered it work—as a school physician on Long Island, where we lived.

Then, after raising my second family to school age and being ready to go to work for the first time, it seemed pure chance that the Planned Parenthood Federation of America offered me the position of medical director. It was as if a whole lot of things finally had come together in this one person, at this one time, for this one job.

Nevertheless, I went into the work with an awareness that, at fifty, I still didn't have the best attitudes about sex, that there still were a lot of hangovers from my childhood. I knew enough not to have marked my daughters in the same way that I had been marked, but not doing something is different from doing something positive. It was just a negative thing. The more I read and the more I became aware of the role sexuality, as a central force, plays in human lives and the more the incredible group of people I encountered through Planned Parenthood began voicing their beliefs, the more aware I was of the enormous implications sexuality has, far beyond teaching children the "facts of life," which is minimal really.

Actually I didn't get much of a chance to deal with the abstract concepts of sexuality at Planned Parenthood. They weren't particularly interested in that. Theirs was more of a mechanical approach to the clinical aspects of birth control, as was appropriate at that time. Meanwhile I had been meeting with a number of colleagues, partly in my capacity as medical director for the organization but also involving various other enterprises more in the ideological realm. Then in 1961 the National Council of Churches convened its first North American Conference on Church and Family. It was an extraordinary conference. It dealt with masturbation, divorce, infidelity, homosexuality—the whole range of sexual behavior. The best researchers of the time presented papers about their special areas.

I had been invited there, to Green Lake, Wisconsin, to speak on planned parenthood, when I suddenly realized that it would be a waste of time; planned parenthood already had been accepted by all the major religious groups. Even the Roman Catholics accepted the principle; it was the method they differed on. So I figured, "Why give them another speech on this? I'm going to speak to the real question, sex education." I did, and it created quite a response. In the aftermath I found myself in frequent contact with many people who, along with me, came to feel more and more strongly that a national sex education council could serve to liberate human sexuality from the fear and ignorance, the guilt and shame, which so often cause people to warp and twist this marvelously important, beautiful, exciting, thrilling faculty we have been given. Many of them became founders and members of the board of SIECUS, the Sex Information and Education Council of the United States, which was founded in 1964 and for which I left Planned Parenthood to accept the position of executive director.

I feel a sense of mission about all this, probably because I am a Quaker. The essence of Quakerism is the concept that God is present in every human being and that if you recognize and speak to that presence your own way will be made more fruitful. I have a sense that this particular road has been laid out for me. People often ask, "Don't you get tired of talking about sex?" How can you get tired of talking about such a marvelous thing? I want to get this message over to help free people from the poisonous leftovers of all our childhoods.

There's so much beauty we try to bury, whether it's about sex or anything else. My primary motivation is to let out what's already there. I'm working for people with regard to their sexuality—for their right to have, and to know, and to be. I really do feel I have been led to this place. It was through a series of chances, good luck, and people—including my husband and daughters—caring enough about me to watch over and bear with me through the years.

Craig Claiborne

FOOD EDITOR

Born in the rural Mississippi delta town of Sunflower in 1920, Craig Claiborne was raised and schooled in Indianola. He graduated from the University of Missouri with a degree in journalism and, after two tours of duty with the U.S. Navy, attended the Professional School of the Swiss Hotelkeepers Association. After working in editorial and public relations positions involving the food industry, he joined The New York Times *in 1957. As food editor he has become one of the newspaper's most famous by-liners and has written eight best-selling books, seven of them cookbooks and one a guide to restaurants.*

My major interest in life is cooking and tasting food. It's an obsession. Writing is secondary, the means of communicating what I feel about food. Even in my childhood I was fascinated watching biscuits being made, but I had no real aspirations to be anything. All the best things that happened to me happened quite late in life. It would have been nice if I had arrived where I am at thirty instead of in my mid-fifties.

My capacity for learning was infinite, provided my teachers would come at me and make me love what they were teaching. But they were negative. They knew nothing about how to get a kid and make him know what beauty is. One of the worst things that ever happened to me was being "bright." My family was so pleased, so flattered by this nonsense, that they skipped me a grade. After that I always was one grade behind in my thinking. I just couldn't catch up. I hope people don't do that anymore. It was just terrible. I had a great lack of ego in almost every aspect of my life. It was an inferiority complex swollen out of all proportion.

At high school in Indianola, Mississippi, every male played football, basketball, or some other sport. I did the things that somehow seemed important to me. I read a lot of Shakespeare. I read the Bible. I read a lot of current novels. Sports just weren't my bag. My freshman mathematics teacher was the football coach, and I was the only boy in the class who didn't sign up. So when he got to my name in calling the roll on the first day, he said, "I see we have a sissy in the class." It was the most embarrassing, humiliating thing in the world. It left an awful scar, the most awful deep wound to this day.

David Sands was one of the salvations of my life. He didn't play football either, but he was a real maverick, an assertive type. David just said, "To hell with them all. I like Thomas Wolfe." And he introduced me to the marvelous works of Wolfe, Emily Dickinson, A. E. Housman, and people like that.

My family always told me that I wanted to be a doctor. So when I

Craig Claiborne: *I really have found a secret in this life. It pays to be audacious. It really helps to be audacious, and sometimes outrageously so.*

graduated from high school I went to Mississippi State College, where I took pre-medical courses. It was just awful. The smell of formaldehyde and the sight of blood made me feel sick to my stomach, and I couldn't stand those pickled frogs. I realized it was not for me at all. In my second year I literally was flunking every course I was taking. I liked to read and I liked to write, though, and I told my family that I wanted to go to the University of Missouri to study journalism. I felt guilty about it, because my family was horrendously poor, all *my* life at least. My father had been a wealthy man, a big plantation owner with an endless number of servants. But he lost everything the year I was born, and my mother, who was a marvelous cook, turned our home into a boardinghouse. Somehow they managed to scratch up the money and send me to Missouri.

Looking back now, it was about $5,000 thrown down the drain. I learned nothing about writing. That's not to the discredit of the university. I am self-willed. I do what I do the way I do it, and that's it. In my case, college actually was detrimental. I do think that, had I taken liberal arts, it would have been fine. Then I would have gained something to use in writing. Not in a mechanical sense. I don't think it's possible to learn how to write. It's a talent you either are born with or not. My early reading was my best preparation. I split my time between Shakespeare and the Bible and read them over and over again. Looking back, I would never have gone to college if I had my way, because I don't think I gained anything from it. All I got was a piece of paper that let me go knocking on doors and say that I had a college degree.

After I graduated in 1942 with a degree from the school of journalism I went directly into the Navy. But it still was with a great sense of insecurity. I had brooded as a child and throughout college and into the Navy about what I would do when I got out into the real world. Although I had my degree I felt incompetent as a writer. I had never written anything serious, but just had dabbled in poetry and written a terribly adolescent play at the university for the drama group. It wasn't accepted.

When the war was over I returned to the university to seek guidance from my former dean. I remember the overwhelming sense of insecurity as I sat in the anteroom of his office thinking, "Maybe I can become a taxi driver or an elevator operator." It seemed as though I would just float for the rest of my life and never be worth a damn at anything. Finally I decided to go to Chicago. A Navy buddy who had gotten out before me had a job there, and there was really nowhere else to go but back to that boardinghouse.

My first job was with a firm that is not aware of the fact that I once worked for them—the Chicago *Daily News*. I worked there for about ten days writing house advertisements. Another Navy buddy who worked directly across the river as assistant director of public relations at the American Broadcasting Company knew how unhappy I was at the paper and called to tell me about an opening at ABC. So I swam the river, so to speak, and started handling publicity for radio programs and personalities, including Don McNeill and his *Breakfast Club* show.

I loved Chicago. It was the first big city I had ever lived in. Other than Memphis, Tennessee, it was the only big town I had ever seen. It also was the first time in my life I had any genuine sense of freedom. I didn't belong to my family, I didn't belong to the Navy, and I didn't have anybody to tell me what to do. But after a while I got bored with all the sundry parts of my life. I had saved about $1,000, and I had the GI bill coming to me in depth. So I decided to run off to Paris and learn French at the Alliance Française.

I've always been a bit of a snob. I came from an enormously arrogant mother, a real *grande dame*, and she instilled some of her arrogance in me. French, I always had heard, was the language of diplomacy, and I had a great illusion that, if I could speak it, all the world would be available to me. The night before I left, all my personal friends and office friends gave me a great party. The next morning I felt they all loved me so much that I was making a terrible mistake, but I forced myself onto the train to New York to catch the boat to Europe. I spent six months in Paris.

All the time I was in Europe I felt I should have been back in Chicago. So that's where I went when I returned to the United States. I joined the Merchandise Mart, again in public relations, and handled such uplifting departments as menswear and children's toys. The job also involved promoting the Merchandise Mart itself, which was the world's largest office building. I had sampled the bouillabaisse at the Merchants and Manufacturers Club in the building. It was very good, and it prompted me to do something which was sort of a turning point in my life because it encouraged me to do something else later.

The food editor on the Chicago *Times* was Ruth Ellen Church, who wrote under the name Mary Meade. I called to ask if she would like to do an article on the chef and his bouillabaisse. She was interested, we met, she wrote the article, and we became casual friends. Shortly after that the Korean War broke out. It was one of the best things that ever happened in my life. I really hated the job of promoting menswear and children's toys, and by then I couldn't stand Chicago for another five minutes. I was living under penurious circumstances to say the least, and I never made more than $5,000 a year until I joined *The New York Times*.

I volunteered to go back into the Navy. It was the first time in my life that I kept my own counsel. I didn't tell anybody. Almost by return mail I got a big brown envelope with my orders. I couldn't wait to see where I was going. I opened it and read, "You are to proceed to the *USS Naiefeh DE352*." I called my boss, Bob Johnson, and with great anguish in my voice said, "Bob, right in mid-career I've been called back into the Navy." He said, "You *what?*" Then, more calmly, he advised, "Don't worry about it. We'll get Sarge Shriver to call Congressman Kennedy. He'll get you out of it." I frankly didn't know who the Kennedys were, even though the family owned the Merchandise Mart. Sargent Shriver, Eunice Kennedy's husband, was assistant manager. Under him was Bob Johnson, as director of promotion and publicity, and then me. The next morning I was scared when I got to work. It would be a fine thing if

Sarge were to get Kennedy on the phone and they then found out that I had volunteered for the very thing they were trying to get me out of. I did a whole lot of triple-talking, no call was made, and I reported aboard the *Naiefeh* in Hawaii.

I had a lot of time to think during my time on that ship. I was thirty-three years old and kept asking myself, "What are you really going to do when you grow up?" It finally came to me that I did have some control over my future; that people do have some choice in this life, more than they believe. I knew that the two things that most appealed to me were foods and writing. This was toward the end of my two-year stretch, and I decided to apply to a cooking school in Switzerland I'd heard of, the Professional School of the Swiss Hotelkeepers Association. They wrote back that I was accepted but that there was a one-year waiting period. I had a small sum of money, but I knew if I got out of the Navy it would be gone by the time the year was up.

So I decided to stay in that great lazy place called the Navy. I didn't have any responsibilities, and it was fun to ride around in a boat. I wrote the Navy to say, "I will be willing to ship over for one year provided you send me to Midway." The *Naiefeh* had stopped there once, and I fell in love with the gooney birds. I loved Midway because of them. By return cable I was told I was to be assigned to Midway as communications officer. The Navy pulled a switch, though, and wound up sending me to Kwajalein, but it turned out to be another of the greatest things that ever happened to me. Before I went I bought myself a copy of the Bible, a complete set of Shakespeare, every Puccini opera I could find, a lot of Verdi, and a tremendous amount of Mozart. I sat for hours and hours on Kwajalein reading those books and listening to music.

After my time was up, I stopped off in Chicago on my way to Switzerland. I called Ruth Ellen Church and reminded her about the article on bouillabaisse. "I'm on my way to a hotel school in Europe," I said. "Would you be interested in seeing some articles from me after I get there?" She said she would, and I later sent her two easy pieces. The first was about breakfasts: what a professional school recommends that hotel managers should have on the menu for American tourists. She bought it and paid me about $35. It was one of the most ecstatic moments in my life. It wasn't the money, but just seeing my name in print.

The school was absolute paradise. The courses in cooking and table service were beautiful. I couldn't believe that I was learning such things, at such a rapid clip too. It became second nature to me. It was an exciting moment to know that I really had found myself at last. I was home safe. I remember once walking across the campus with John Sihler, who now owns a restaurant in Chicago. John asked me what I wanted to do when I got out of there. It was just making talk, but I told him, "I want to be food editor of *The New York Times*."

I had been in New York about four days when I got back to America, and I called Jane Nickerson, the food editor of the *Times*. One thing my public relations training taught me is what you can and cannot get by with, and you can get by with an awful lot. I said, "Miss Nickerson, you don't know me, but would you like to write an article about a young American who knows all about classic French cooking?" She said she would and asked, "Who is it?" I told her, "It is I. I just came back from a hotel school in Switzerland, and I finished with fairly high grades." So we went to lunch, and the first thing I said to her was, "You know, you have the one job in the world I want." She interviewed me and went back and wrote a marvelous article.

I had met the food establishment. Then I went to *Gourmet* magazine to get some advice. I met the managing editor, Ann Seranne, and after we spoke awhile she suggested that I see Claude Phillippe at the Waldorf-Astoria. That proved useless, and a week later I went back to see her again. It was a Friday afternoon, and I know she was just trying to get rid of me when she asked if I would like to try writing an article for *Gourmet*. Bloody Marys were coming into popularity then, and she suggested a piece on vodka. I rented a typewriter for the weekend and went to the library to do the research. Monday morning I walked in with the article. She just flipped, paid me $350, and I couldn't believe it. Then she asked if I would like to do another, on tea. I was back with it on Friday, and she paid me another $350. I did still another, and Ann said she would like to hire me. This was in May, and the job wouldn't be available until October—and then just as receptionist. So determined was I, though, to get into this funny field of writing about foods that I went to the nearest employment office for a temporary job to tide me over. They had just one opening, for a waiter to double as bartender at a place called the Bobbin' Inn near Nyack, New York. I got on a bus and went up there.

The next months were the worst in my life. I had to sleep above the restaurant right through the middle of summer, under a tin roof with terrible sunlight beating down on it all day and no ventilation. I was mixing cocktails, jumping over the bar and serving, and then back behind the bar. It was so tiring that, with the restaurant closed on Mondays, I would catch a late bus on Sunday nights, check into a room at the Hotel Roosevelt in Manhattan, and stay in bed until I had to go back to work again.

In October I shipped on as receptionist at *Gourmet*. The job essentially involved opening the mail, answering the telephone, and replying to reader correspondence. As it turned out, articles for which I used to get $350 I was writing gratis. Ann would have paid me for them if she could have. We were very close and very fond of each other and respected each other. She was a highly creative person, a fantastic talent. She finally left and opened her own public relations firm. I went with her, but I still had this sordid lack of ego.

My mother, who is dead now, came to New York once and gave me $100 to go to a psychiatrist. I deeply resented that. I always had this love-hate relationship with my mother, an intense love-hate relationship which leaned more to hate. In fact, I am convinced, after psychiatry, that my aggressiveness in pursuing my career was purely and simply to prove that I could do any bloody damn thing my mother could do and do it ten times better. She was well known throughout Mississippi for her cooking. She also had a great command of the language, a marvelous style—nothing professional, but her letters were masterpieces.

I took the money and went to an analyst. He couldn't take me because he didn't have an opening and said that $100 wouldn't get me very much anyhow. But he did recommend that I go to the Payne Whitney Clinic at New York Hospital. I did, and after an interview the doctor said he would take me on, beginning the next day. It was really fantastic. I was paying about $1 a week, and great things, just phenomenal things, started happening in my life.

Jane Nickerson had told the *Times* she was leaving. Her husband had to go to Florida because of his job, and she and the children were left in New York. She didn't want the separation. That was toward the end of the summer of 1957.

Ann Seranne had suggested that we take Jane to lunch. We did, and Jane started to elaborate on the vast number of people who were parading through *The New York Times* in search of her job. The wheels started turning in my brain. I thought it certainly wouldn't hurt if I applied. I had nothing to lose. That was an astonishing moment in my life, because with my great lack of ego I normally never would have thought of applying for the job, but I went back to the office, closed the door, and wrote an impassioned letter telling Jane how much I loved the *Times*. Which was true; I had tremendous respect for the paper. I recapped my background and sent the letter off. Ten days passed. Then Jane called. "I don't want to get your hopes up," she said, "but the *Times* is interested in talking with you." Next I got a call from Elizabeth Penrose Howkins, who was the women's editor. We went to lunch, and she appeared to be impressed, but there was great tension about the possibility of me getting the job. The editor of the Sunday magazine at that time had a particular woman in mind for the job. Other people didn't like her, but he was a powerful influence.

After having lunch with Elizabeth Howkins, I stopped in to see the managing editor, Turner Catledge. He was from Mississippi. I knew too that he had gone to Mississippi State and that he had stayed in Polecat Alley, the same dormitory section as I had. He asked, "Where did you go to college, son?" In my best Southern accent I said, "Mississippi State College." He asked, "Where did you stay?" I said, "Polecat Alley," and he said, "So did I, son." So we talked, and he finally said, "I like you, son. I think you'll be good for the job." I replied, "You know there's an awful lot of opposition to my coming here." He said, "I do the hiring and firing." I still didn't have my hopes up when I left.

I went on vacation to Fire Island and was walking the beach one morning when I got a call. It was *The New York Times*. The job was mine provided I passed the physical. I took the train back to town that afternoon, took the physical, and came back that night. The next day, the *Times* called again and said I was to start in September.

I'll never forget that morning, walking the beach and thinking, "What can I write about?" Then I saw a man catching a bluefish, and I thought, "I'll write about bluefish." Then I thought, "What will I do the following week?" It was silly speculation, and somehow it's all come along. It has been with a great heroic effort at times that I've done some of the things I've done. But I really have found a secret in this life. It pays to be audacious. It really helps to be audacious, and sometimes outrageously so.

Kenneth B. Clark

SOCIAL PSYCHOLOGIST

Born in the Panama Canal Zone in 1914, Dr. Kenneth B. Clark attended public schools in New York City and received his bachelor's and master's degrees from Howard University and his Ph.D. from Columbia University. He is a Distinguished Professor of Psychology Emeritus of the City University of New York, where he was a faculty member of the psychology department for more than thirty years. His work contributed to the 1954 ruling by the U.S. Supreme Court that school segregation is unconstitutional. He founded and headed Harlem Youth Opportunities Unlimited, a precursor of the White House's war on poverty, and is past president of the American Psychological Association and of the Metropolitan Applied Research Center. He currently is president of Clark, Phipps, Clark & Harris, which counsels business and institutions on human relations, race relations, and affirmative action programs. He is a member of the Board of Regents of the State of New York and a member of the Board of Trustees of the University of Chicago.

I always enjoyed school and admired my good teachers. One of the reasons I ended up teaching is because I so admired them. All the teachers I respected had in common the ability to take their particular subject matter and give it a perspective, an order, a meaning. They made ideas come to life. They also set standards. They would not accept shoddy work, and I did not respect the teachers who did.

My mother set that standard for me too. She would not accept race or color as alibis, either as excuses for inferior performance or as insurmountable barriers. It was the one message with which she bludgeoned me and my sister. She was aware of racial prejudice and discrimination. She didn't tell us to pretend they didn't exist, but she wouldn't let them shackle us. She just said, "Look, to hell with it. Whatever anyone else can do, you can do." That's what I later told my children and what they tell theirs.

My mother and father were from Jamaica, but with the building of the Panama Canal their families migrated to the Canal Zone for economic reasons. That's where my mother and father met, and they lived there until my mother left my father in 1918, when I was four years old. She came to New York like most immigrants, seeking a better way of life but also escaping my father and the problems he posed. Judging from my correspondence with him, my father—who is now dead—was an arrogant man. I am sure my mother's leaving him was a very positive influence on my life. He would not have been as totally supportive as she was.

He had a good job in Panama as superintendent of cargo with the United Fruit Company. It was quite something for a black man to have a white-collar job, and his father had had the same job before him. But my mother felt, and rightly so, that if we stayed in Panama the most she could look forward to for her son would be to follow in their footsteps. She was and still is a very firm, forthright, and ambitious woman, and that didn't satisfy her. She knew what she wanted—particularly for her children. She wanted us to have edu-

Kenneth B. Clark: *Selfish pursuits are easy, but life is not worth much if spent on that.*

cational opportunities and the ability to advance.

When we arrived in New York she got a job in a garment factory and worked there until she retired in the 1960s. Single-handedly she saw me and my sister—who was three years younger—through college and into graduate school. She stimulated my sister and me to improve ourselves, and she earned her high school diploma at George Washington High School—the same school I attended—by going nights.

Aside from my mother, my teachers always were my most positive influences. I still have in my mind rather clear, vivid images of significant teachers throughout my school days—from elementary school through college. I can see them smiling—Miss Maguire, Mr. Deegan, Miss Smith, Mr. Mitchell. I especially remember a junior high school speech teacher, Mr. Dixon, who was the first person to indicate to me that I could take ideas and transform them into words in which other people would be interested. He had me give a three-minute speech one day and was very positive in his reaction to it. I didn't understand what was so special about it, but he continued to draw me out. He had me enter an essay contest sponsored by Bond Bread. I don't remember what I wrote about, but I gave it to him and he turned it in, and I won a gold medal. I was very proud when I received it during an assembly period, and Mr. Dixon was proud too. I don't know why it is, but I remember the names of only the teachers I admired. I have been able to block out the others.

There was a guidance counselor in junior high school who tried to direct me to a vocational high school. I do not remember that woman's name. She had the feeling that black students—we were called "colored" then—should be realistic and not go on to academic schools. I suppose she was in the vanguard of counselors who interpreted their roles as protecting us from frustration and unhappiness by shunting us off to meaningless vocational schools, which were of a lower status than academic schools. She was persistent about it, but my mother took care of her. I was in the room the day my mother stormed in and said to her, "I don't care where you send your son, but mine is going to George Washington High School." My mother was not in any way awed by authority, and I think that saved my sister and me.

The only other bad memory I have is of an economics teacher, although he was a good teacher. I was the best student in his class, and he determined who would get the economics prize at the high school graduation. I was shocked and so were my classmates when, even though I deserved it, it went to someone else. Frankly, he wasn't ready at that time to award it to a black student.

My mother's dream was for me to become an Episcopal priest, but I had no illusions about priests and the priesthood, for the simple reason that I had been an altar boy from the time I was six until I was sixteen and went to college. During high school I decided I wanted to become a physician. I guess that came from observing the status and prestige physicians seemed to have. But also I had a crafts teacher at a summer playground who was a medical student at Howard University in Washington, D.C. She was very attractive, and I admired her so much I decided I wanted to go to Howard. That turned out to be the most influential decision to affect my future career.

Throughout my freshman year and part of my sophomore year at Howard, I took all the pre-medical courses I could—biology, chemistry, physics. Then as a luxury I registered for an introductory course in psychology for the second half of my sophomore year. Dr. Francis Cecil Sumner taught it, and as I listened to this man I heard a wisdom, a comprehensive view of man in society, an attempt to deal rationally and systematically with human problems—human dignity. I don't know whether or not it was at any given moment, but as I listened and listened I decided I was not going to go to medical school; that I was going to pursue the study of psychology. Dr. Sumner, without being aware of it, had made it clear to me that that was probably the most important area in which human intelligence should be involved.

Other things happening to me in my sophomore year supported

me in that choice. I remember the day in chemistry lab when a senior who was working close-by showed me the letter of admission to medical school he had received that morning. Paradoxically, that incident confirmed my intent not to go to medical school. It put the finishing touch on my decision, because I had seen him cheating on exams. I did not respect him, and it seemed to me that almost anybody could go to medical school. It perhaps was unfair, but I had seen other classmates too doing almost anything to get the grades they needed to gain admission to medical school. But that only confirmed the decision Dr. Sumner's influence had led me to make. He became my intellectual father, my friend, my adviser, my confidant, and from my sophomore year on everything in my choice of courses converged around my primary interest in psychology. No teacher before or since ever had the impact he had. He was totally supportive.

I've been very fortunate in the positive influences the significant people in my life have had on me—including my wife, who was a freshman at Howard when I was a senior. I remember when, as a freshman, she said, "Kenneth, one of these days you're going to be a great psychologist." I took it just as courtship talk, but she always believed it, and that was a great support.

The shift to psychology gave a great deal of meaning to my life. I saw psychology as a systematic, rational use of human intelligence, not only to understand social problems but to help in finding answers to them. Although my primary activity throughout my career has been as an academician, my laboratory always was society, the social environment. My involvement in various social issues was never in competition or conflict with my academic role but was quite compatible with it. I never regarded the academic role—particularly in the social sciences—as one which can be fulfilled in isolation.

As I look back on my experiences as an undergraduate at Howard University during the 1930s, I am convinced that my philosophy of the social role of disciplined human intelligence was being skillfully shaped by significant teachers. In addition to Dr. Sumner, such professors as Alvin L. Locke, Ralph Bunche, E. Franklin Frazier, Sterling Brown, and a few others not only taught me subject matter in the classroom but became my counselors and friends. They were my models and they identified with me, encouraged me, and advised me in the early stages of my academic career. If Dr. Sumner was my intellectual father, they were my intellectual godfathers, who made social sensitivity an integral part of all of my work as a social psychologist.

After I graduated from Howard I decided to stay on studying with Dr. Sumner to get my master's degree, which I received at the end of the next year. He then kept me on to teach with him. That was quite an honor, but he soon encouraged me to go for my Ph.D., and I agreed. I applied to just two schools—Cornell and Columbia. Cornell wrote back and said they were sorry but, since Ph.D. candidates worked so closely together, they couldn't admit me because I was black. It was a stupid letter, and I was angry. I don't believe I answered it, but if I did I would have told them I was planning to go there to learn—not to socialize. I wish I had saved that letter, but every time I have gone to Cornell to give a talk I've been mean enough to remind them of it.

Columbia did accept me, and I was glad because Dr. Otto Klineberg was there. I had heard him speak when he lectured at Howard while I was a graduate student, and he and his ideas impressed me. I enjoyed Columbia and speaking with the professors both inside and outside of class. Dr. Sumner had prepared me so well for the Ph.D. work, it was almost leisurely. During my studies at Columbia I also worked with Gunnar Myrdal, the Swedish sociologist and economist. Dr. Klineberg had recommended me to him, and the work consisted of studying and synthesizing the psychological literature on race. Also, my wife and I were doing research on racial awareness of children, but even that, as far as we were concerned, was pure research. It was for her master's thesis at Howard, and we conceived of it as an abstract problem. We had no such intent at the time, but it later became an important component of social policy and social change. I wasn't aware of it, but everything I was doing was preparing me for my involvement in the 1950s with the *Brown* decision by which the U.S. Supreme Court declared school segregation unconstitutional.

After I received my Ph.D. and completed my work with Myrdal, I taught for a while at Hampton Institute, a black college in Virginia. I left there within a year and went into the Office of War Information, where in 1941–42 I was involved in a study of the morale of blacks in America. Then in 1943 I joined the psychology department of the College of the City of New York and stayed there until I retired from teaching in 1975. The whole experience of teaching was a thrilling, stimulating, growing experience. You cannot teach without learning, and I don't recall a single class I had in all the years of teaching in which I didn't learn something. My wife would say to me, "You know, with all these other things you're doing, the real thing you enjoy—the thing you really thrive on—is teaching." She was right, because Dr. Sumner, a person whose life was devoted to teaching, was my model. I could go into a classroom with a headache or a cold, and within ten or fifteen minutes I was feeling wonderful. I remember ten or twelve of my students from all those years as vividly as I remember my teachers. I remember them not because of a surface brilliance or because they could write excellent papers. They went beyond that. They brought to their studies a passionate sensitivity, and a critical probing intelligence.

The action part of my career didn't surface until 1950. The lawyers of the NAACP had gone to Dr. Klineberg for guidance as to how psychologists could help them on school segregation cases. He referred them to me because he knew of the work I had been doing on racial awareness and the effects of prejudice, discrimination, and segregation on personality development in children. From that point on my life was changed because I got involved with those cases on the trial level.

There were five cases—in Delaware, Kansas, South Carolina,

Virginia, and the District of Columbia. My involvement was as a social scientist testifying on the effects of discrimination and segregation and helping to write a brief, which was a social science brief, for submission to the Supreme Court. The Supreme Court's decision that segregation in schools was in violation of the Fourteenth Amendment was a highlight of my career. My immediate reaction was one of regret that Dr. Sumner—who had died of a heart attack—was not there to share my pleasure in being involved with that decision.

When it comes right down to it, I guess the principal guideline—one which people important to me throughout my life have helped me to establish and which I have tried to follow—is the sense of the personal worth and substance of every individual. Everything else converges on that. The work my wife does at the Northside Center for Child Development, which we founded, is an acting out of that belief. So was our work with Harlem Youth Opportunities Unlimited and the Metropolitan Applied Research Center. It is what I tried to tell my students. It is what I try to say in my books. It is what I try to communicate to my children and grandchildren—that no human being is expendable and that we have a responsibility to our fellow human beings. Selfish pursuits are easy, but life is not worth much if spent on that.

Judith Crist

FILM CRITIC

At the age of twelve, when her family returned to the United States after living in Canada, Judith Crist fully discovered movies for the first time and shortly thereafter decided her career goal was to become a movie critic. Currently the film reviewer for the New York Post *and* TV Guide, *she graduated from the Columbia University School of Journalism in 1945. She then joined the New York* Herald-Tribune, *where she won a number of awards for general reporting before becoming the paper's award-winning movie critic eighteen years later. From 1963 to 1973 she was film and drama critic on NBC-TV's* Today Show; *she was film critic for* New York *magazine from its inception in 1968 until 1975; and film critic for* Saturday Review *from 1975 to 1977. A poll conducted by Louis Harris Associates found her to be regarded as the most influential film critic in the United States, and she twice has served as the elected chairman of the New York Film Critics Circle. She is an adjunct professor at the Columbia School of Journalism, where she has been a member of the working faculty since 1959.*

I grew up in a very verbal family. My mother had been a New York City librarian until my father dropped out of school shortly after their marriage and decided he was going to make his fortune as a fur trader. That was about eight businesses before I was born, and they landed in Canada. My father was a literate man and somewhat of a romantic adventurer—a year of law school here, a year of medical school there, and "No, no. You can become a millionaire much more easily this way."

There were four of us—my parents, my brother, and I—and it was a story-filled family. After dinner each evening one of us would read a chapter of Dickens or Thackeray while my parents had their coffee. During summers my mother and I often would sit under a shady tree in the fields and read aloud to each other. I always thought I would be a writer of some kind, and by the time we returned to the United States when I was twelve I had written a lot of chapters for the Great American Novel.

Movies were a much-forbidden fruit in Canada. In Toronto, where we lived briefly, they were available to us youngsters only on Saturday afternoons. In Montreal you were not allowed to go to the movies, except for special kiddy shows, until you were sixteen. When we moved back to New York in the 1930s I became an absolute movie maniac. There were double features to be seen three times a week at each neighborhood movie house, and I just fell in love with film. To me movies were the ultimate in storytelling and became all-absorbing. I chose to think that the real world was there in the dark and the rest of life just was something you had to get through. During high school and college I got in all the movie-going I possibly could.

The film critics I read as an adolescent in the late 1930s were Otis Ferguson in the *New Republic*, James Agee in *The Nation*, and Frank Nugent in *The New York Times*. Those three were major influences on me. The first woman critic I encountered was Cecilia

Judith Crist: *It shows how near-sighted a person can be. My dream was coming true right in front of me, and I didn't recognize what was happening.*

Ager, who wrote for *PM*, the daily newspaper which began publishing around 1940, and by then I had my sights set on movie criticism. It was a rather venal ambition, because it had dawned on me that if you were a movie critic you could get to see all the movies ever made; you would get to see them for nothing; and you would get to see them on company time. Movie criticism was not a very respectable occupation, however. So I did think more formally of theater and literary criticism while I was at Hunter College. In the back of my mind, though, was the full intention of becoming a movie critic—respectable or not.

As a senior at Hunter, where I majored in English with a minor in education, I invited Frank Nugent to come and speak to the English Club, of which I was president. It was with a very ulterior motive. He wrote to say he was sorry but he could not come because he was resigning his job to go to Hollywood and suggested that Bosley Crowther, who was to succeed him at the *Times*, would be a most rewarding speaker. So Mr. Crowther came instead, and a week after graduation I showed up at the *Times* to ask, "Remember me?" I offered him a proposition. I said I would sharpen his pencils, retype his articles—I was that naïve—and practically shine his shoes and wash his floors if he would let me go to the movies with him and if he then would criticize my reviews. He kept a perfectly straight face and said, "I believe in the apprentice system, and there is nothing I would like better. But we do have a union here, and I would not be able to employ you without a salary. Since we have no budget for that, my advice to you, if you are interested in newspaper criticism, is to find a regular job on a newspaper."

I never forgot the extreme kindness and graciousness with which Bosley treated me. I was glad to be able to thank him twenty-two years later when I—as the newly appointed movie critic of the New York *Herald-Tribune*—was introduced to him at a screening of *Cleopatra*.

I was in the great class of 1941 at Hunter (Bella Abzug, Regina Resnick, Pearl Primus—just for starters). The war disrupted all our lives. Eventually I wound up as a civilian instructor with the 3081st Army Air Force Base Unit. I taught a pre-preflight training course in military communications, which in peacetime would have been called English grammar. It was to teach men who were college graduates how to write and speak as officers and gentlemen. As the need for pilots, navigators, and bombardiers lessened in the spring of 1944, the course became a therapeutic thing. We began getting ground troops and air crewmen who had been in combat. Many of them had not gotten past the sixth grade, and they were the most memorable. The experience was the most important thing that ever happened to me, because I came to understand that you could have gone to school for only six years—in Tennessee, Alabama, or Georgia—and still be a rewarding and intelligent human being. Those of my generation who had gone to an academic high school in New York during the Depression and then through college were typical elitists. We did not think other people—let alone anyone west of the Hudson River—had any value. If you couldn't quote T.S. Eliot you weren't worth talking to. It was the ultimate snobbery of the East.

After the Air Force experience, I decided journalism was to be my path to movie criticism, and I entered the Columbia University Graduate School of Journalism. When I was graduated in 1945 the *Herald-Tribune* was the best newspaper in the country, and the women's editor, Dorothy Dunbar Bromley, had told Columbia she was looking for a reporter. The administration did not send me to see her, because they regarded me as a rather independent, mature person who could find her own job, and indeed I had.

I had seen an ad in *Editor & Publisher,* placed by a former city editor of *The New York Times* who wanted a reporter for his newspaper in Petersburg, West Virginia. It sounded quite glowing, and I went down there for an interview. This ex-editor of the *Times* was a marvelous man who had built up a lovely weekly. The war was ending—it was May—and he was going to convert the paper into a daily as soon as things settled down. He offered me a car of my own, an assistant, $50 a week, and the promise of a 50 percent share in the paper if we got along for about five years. I came back to New York—and May and October are magical months to me as an almost lifelong New Yorker—and when I caught the glitter and the sparkle in the air, I thought, "I must be insane. I don't want to go to West Virginia." Besides, I had looked back at the station as I was boarding the train in Petersburg and seen the restroom doors marked "White" and "Colored"—and the same signs on the drinking fountains—and I already had started to think, "My God, I couldn't."

A few days later I passed the *Herald-Tribune* on my way home from shopping at Macy's. I thought, "The school didn't send me, but that's the best job around and I would like to have it." So on sheer impulse I went up, applied, and had an interview with Dorothy Bromley. I also was considering another job which was open. *The New Yorker* magazine had told Columbia they were looking for a *man* editorial assistant. That burned me. I knew Morris Ernst, the lawyer for the magazine, and he was enough of a civil libertarian to offer to recommend me for the job that was fit only for a man. I went to meet him at the Biltmore Hotel to discuss it. He was on his way to Nantucket for the Memorial Day weekend and was going to grab a train from Grand Central Station. I had with me a bundle of material I was going to send to Dorothy Bromley in follow-up to the interview. He asked me what it was, and when I told him he said, "Dorothy Bromley! I know her. Give me a piece of paper." He took my letter to her and wrote on the back, "Dorothy, you're a fool if you don't hire this girl. Call me in Nantucket." The Tuesday after that weekend, she called and said, "Judith, this is Dorothy Bromley. When can you come to work?"

If the *Tribune* had not eventually gone under I would be there to this day. It was my favorite home. It was not long to remain the newspaperman's paper it was then, and it went through some very seedy times, but when John Hay Whitney bought it in 1960 it was for the next six years a remarkably fine paper.

I was somewhat distressed when I arrived at the *Tribune*, because it was obvious I was not going to become a movie critic overnight. In fact, it took me some eighteen years. I started on what was called the "Sunday Woman's Page," which all the men in the office called the Social Significance Page. Dorothy Bromley, I, and a number of other people were what the more cynical called "bleeding hearts." Dorothy had created a marvelous page of social issues from what had been a bunch of women's club notices. The one gimmick was that we had to find women to tag the articles onto, and we did. The page had been going for two years when I got there. After about five years altogether, the Sunday "Review of the Week" section absorbed it, and I wound up on the city staff.

Reporters could write additional pieces for Sunday sections, and Walter Terry, the dance critic, was the first person ever to give me the opportunity to write a review. He was going to be away and asked me to cover a performance of the Ballet de Paris. I did occasional book reviews too, and—without owning a television set— I did interviews with producers and actors of hit TV shows. After I owned a television set, I found it was much harder to write those pieces with enthusiasm. The critics and I became great chums. We had a Friday lunch club which consisted of myself; Otis Guernsey, the drama editor, who had been the movie critic; Bill Zinsser, Otis's successor as movie critic, who later became a columnist; and Walter Terry.

Everybody knew I was interested in reviewing movies, and a few times when he was short-handed Otis gave me minor movies to review. I wanted more than that, but the editors kept telling me, "It's not the right time." They were quite right, because I was as opinionated and far more rigid than either Otis or Bill, each of whom had come a cropper with the advertisers. I would not have lasted long with my outspoken way, because there was not a newspaper in the country that would stand up to the big movie companies if a critic offended them. Bill Zinsser, in fact, was made a columnist after he wrote a movie review that offended Twentieth Century–Fox, and Otis had become drama editor for the same reason. The *Tribune* very politely shifted critics to other jobs. Other papers shafted them.

Another factor working against me was that I was a very good reporter. When a critic went on vacation, the news editors chose the least valuable reporters to fill in, because they could afford to spare them. On lesser papers, outside New York, when it was the off-season for basketball, the basketball writer would review the movies. He then would yield to the baseball writer. The news editors even in New York regarded drama and movies as fringe departments, and they said to me, "Why do you want to bury yourself in a fringe department?" I was a good writer and very fast. I did general-assignment stories. I was at the national conventions—and not to do women's articles. I did financial stories. I did scandals and crime. There was nothing I didn't cover.

By 1957, however, I had established myself sufficiently that I actually was able to use my value as a reporter in order to get to do reviews. I knew movies still were too risky for me under the then publisher of the paper. So I approached the editor and told him I wanted to review Off-Broadway shows. I said I would be much happier as a general-assignment reporter if I could do that in addition to my regular work. I also pointed out that I would be better at it than the guy who was doing it at the time. It was ruthless, but I always have believed what a teacher once told us at Hunter College. She said, "He who hath a horn and tooteth it not shall die untooted." I also made my calculated approach to the editor because I was married and had a child whom I was away from too much. (One day when I returned after almost two weeks of covering the British royal family's tour of Canada, my son stood up in his crib, turned to me, and said, "Bye-bye." Then he turned to his nurse and said, "Momma.")

So I began doing Off-Broadway reviews. Two years later when Jock Whitney bought the paper, my son was three years old, and I was even more conscious of my maternal responsibilities. I turned down the opportunity to cover Khrushchev's tour of the United

States and said I really needed a more regular job at the paper. Jock Whitney and Fendall Yerxa, the editor he had brought in, proposed that I edit the "Lively Arts" section. We turned the traditional Sunday drama section into a new tabloid section that consolidated the various arts—dance, movies, drama, music, television, and so on. I became the editor, but with the provision that I could continue to review Off-Broadway shows. Intent as I was on becoming a movie critic, I was very deep into theater at that time.

I always have had a very bad tendency to become so engrossed in the immediacy of a situation that I don't pull back and look at it. Therefore, I did not connect this new assignment with the possible opportunity it presented for doing movie reviews. So I edited the "Lively Arts" section for two years until the famous newspaper strike in 1962.

That strike was completely different from previous ones. It left New York City without a single newspaper for four months, and the radio and television stations rushed in to fill the void. As editor of the "Lively Arts" section at the *Tribune*, I was asked to appear on this program and that program to review plays and movies. I was on the eleven o'clock night news and seven o'clock morning news on ABC and doing a lot of other reviewing. I created quite a stir, and that's when the NBC *Today Show* spotted me. It was very, very heady—a sudden glamorous career—and at the end of the strike I was invited to stay on in television. I had developed a romantic love affair with journalism, though, and came back to the *Tribune* toward the end of the strike to consult with the then editor, Jim Bellows, and Jock Whitney about starting up the paper again.

We already had begun a search for a new movie critic just before the strike. The reviews we had been printing were bland, and the advertisers were unhappy—not because of the tone of the reviews, which usually were quite favorable, but because the reviewer wasn't being read. So the movie companies felt their ads were not seen. When I went back, Bellows and Whitney said they had reached a decision about a movie critic. They wanted me to take it. My immediate reaction was, "Why? Don't you think I am the most absolutely perfect editor for the arts?" It shows how near-sighted a person can be. My dream was coming true right in front of me, and I didn't recognize what was happening. Finally I said okay and in all vanity assured them that in six months they would have the best movie critic in the city and within a year the best movie critic in the country.

Jock Whitney is ever to be remembered for bringing true moral character to the role of publisher. We had a *cause célèbre* about the loss of advertising when I offended Warner Brothers with my review of *Spencer's Mountain.* Jock Whitney and Jim Bellows defended me as the *Tribune's* critic—right or wrong. It was the first time a newspaper ever defended a critic editorially. It drew national attention and, because of that, film criticism—which had been extremely vulnerable because of the amount of advertising in-volved—achieved new status.

My first review was of a Peter Sellers movie, *The Wrong Arm of the Law,* and half of it got lost in the composing room. Instead of eight paragraphs, only four appeared in the paper. Nobody said, "What happened? It seemed to stop in the middle." That taught me a lot about long-winded writing. I have learned shorter is better— not necessarily writing about less, but saying things more succinctly. For instance, I devoted seven columns to *Cleopatra* and four and a half columns to *Doctor Zhivago,* but in the long eye of movie history each perhaps deserves just the thirty-five words they ultimately got in the reviews I did for *TV Guide* when they ran on television.

The notion that the critic is the voice of God, the absolute discern-er of truth, is a view held by only a few fascist critics. It's a view not generally shared, certainly not by mature critics with a sense of proportion and a sense of humor, which many cineastes and critics seem to lack. Maybe the one thing a critic does is establish who that critic is and what the critic's standards and tastes are. Knowing that, the reader can know if that critic is his agent or not. Bosley Crowther and I vividly demonstrated that once, although not by intent. We each had reviewed a Simone Signoret movie, and Bosley described it as the story of a nymphomaniac. I said it was the story of a mature woman. That told a lot more about Bosley and me than it did about the movie.

As a mass-entertainment medium, movies are a sociological reflection of their time. I long ago came to the conclusion that if you see the movies of a nation, you will know what that nation and its people truly are. Yet I don't think I ever was guilty of taking movies too seriously, and that's something I have to guard against constantly. *Star Wars* absolutely delighted and utterly charmed me. I came away with a silly smile on my face. It was refreshing and sweet and good and kind and magical. They all lived happily ever after, and it was Saturday afternoon all over again—Saturday afternoon at the movies, which was the most purely ecstatic time of our lives. However, it's comparative, and to say it's the greatest of its kind is the delusion you can have in the movies. That is the pitfall you have to keep reminding yourself of. Just as the worst movie isn't the worst ever, as you'll find out three days later. It took me about five years to learn not to use the word "masterpiece." Film is still a very new medium—less than a hundred years old—and nobody really knows its full potential.

I feel that I have had a great advantage, because there is hardly an element of the real world dealt with in film which I have not encountered. My personal experiences, including those as wife and mother, have been just as important as all my journalistic experiences. One of the unfortunate things about contemporary film criticism is that too many kids come right out of the college film society and go smack into the professional screening room without ever living a little and experiencing life in between.

Walter Cronkite

CBS NEWS CORRESPONDENT

Born in St. Joseph, Missouri, Walter Cronkite grew up first in Kansas City, Missouri, and then, from age ten, in Houston, Texas, where his father accepted a teaching position at the University of Texas dental school. He attended the university himself until his junior year, when he took a full-time job in journalism. After several years of going between print and broadcast journalism, he spent eleven years with United Press before joining CBS in 1950. He has covered virtually every major news event since joining CBS and has conducted many head-line-making interviews with leading world figures. National polls have found him to be both the single most trusted public figure and most objective newscaster in America. Among the many honors he has received are a number of Emmy awards and major citations from the International Radio and Television Society, the National Press Club, the National Academy of Television Arts and Sciences, and the George Polk Memorial Award Committee.

I had brief flirtations with the idea of becoming a lawyer, an Episcopal minister, and a mining engineer, but they all were temporary aberrations. Journalism is the only thing I remember ever thinking seriously about from the time I was twelve.

It might have had to do with a series of short stories that ran in *American Boy* magazine. They were dramatizations of various careers, and the two which struck me as most interesting were journalism and mining engineering. I just barely held mining engineering in the back of my mind for two or three years, but I got into journalism right away. Actually I'm not sure which really came first—the chicken or the egg—because I was already working on my junior high school newspaper in Houston. It wasn't much of a paper, and I didn't do much on it, but I liked it.

I got very active on my high school paper, and a molding process took place there. We had a marvelous journalism teacher named Fred Birney, and he was superb in providing career guidance. We had more than two thousand students in the school, and we turned out a weekly that was very good—a real newspaper of four to eight pages. We did the page make-up, the dummies, the whole thing. We spent one night a week at the printer's putting it to bed, and I eventually became editor.

During the summers of my junior and senior high school years I also worked as a cub reporter for the Houston *Post*. Each summer the paper took on at no pay—the Newspaper Guild hadn't come along yet—two or three people interested in journalism. The *Post* paid our carfare and assigned us to cover things like Rotary and Kiwanis Club luncheons, so we also got free lunches. It was a very nice little apprenticeship, and we learned something about the newspaper business. The summer before college I went early to the University of Texas as campus correspondent for the *Post*, which paid me space rates. I also got a paid job on the *Daily Texan*, the university student newspaper.

Walter Cronkite: *During those first three or four years out of school when I was bouncing between print and broadcasting, it really was a case of finding myself— experimenting. I'm glad now that I did, because I think it was all for the better.*

My major was in political science and economics because the university didn't have a degree in journalism at that time, but even then I think I had a certain distrust of journalism schools. Although I wanted to be a journalist, I didn't feel the formal education of classes in journalism was what I needed. I thought there were broader areas in education which would serve me better. I still think students spend too much time studying the techniques of being news people and too little time getting a broad academic education. Also, I was a little egotistical then about my journalistic abilities because I felt my experience exceeded that of most of the freshmen around me. As I got into the real world of journalism, though, the egotism faded, and by the time I was overseas in World War II I certainly didn't think of myself as one of the great foreign correspondents, one of the great writers. But I sensed stories, I saw them faster than most.

I did take some freshman courses at the university in news writing and page make-up, but they were pretty simple stuff. Fred Birney was way ahead of them with what he had taught us in high school, and I already had learned a lot by writing for the *Post*.

Radio interested me too. I especially admired Kern Tipps, a dashing figure who was a newscaster at KTRH in Houston and who also was the sports editor of the Houston *Chronicle*. I thought the most glamorous job in the world would be to do dance-band re-motes. It was a childish fascination from listening to announcers who stood at their microphones in front of the bands and said, "From high above Michigan Avenue in downtown Chicago . . ." In fact, I got to do one or two of those on local radio while I was still in high school, just by hanging around the fancy resorts in Galveston.

While at the university I tried out at KTUT. I just went in and asked if they had anything, because I needed the money and was scrambling everywhere looking for jobs. Radio was terribly informal in 1933 because it still was pioneering, and the station hired me for $1 a day to do a five-minute evening sportscast on baseball scores. It was a little thing, but fascinating.

The station had no incoming information of its own because it couldn't afford a baseball ticker. But we were located on the ground floor of the Driskill Hotel, and right up the alley from the back door of the hotel was a beer parlor with a Western Union ticker. It also had a blackboard on which they wrote the scores of the major games as they came in, and I'd rush down there and stand with a Coke or something while I memorized the scores. I figured, if anyone saw me writing them down, Western Union or someone would complain. Then just before going on the air I'd quickly run up the alley, writing down the scores, and do the newscast. I amplified considerably on the basic information I had, using my imagination to describe what was happening on the field. I did other occasional announcing too, including a couple of morning hillbilly-music shows when the regular announcer didn't show up.

Harfield Wheeden was the station manager at KTUT. He was a young man, not much older than I, but I looked up to him considerably. He once told me I should stick to print—that I never would make it in broadcasting. He's now a CBS vice-president, and I never cease to kid him about it when we meet at network conventions.

Within that first couple of years I moved quickly ahead of my contemporaries, because I knew I wanted journalism. The others just were playing at it, but I threw all my energies into it and jumped a quantum distance ahead. I did a lot of reading about journalism and became an expert on the lore of foreign correspondents. I think it was Joseph Anthony who compiled collections of outstanding news stories of the year during the 1920s. I read them all, and I practiced journalism all the time with a dedication of purpose. Even while working on the paper in high school, I put out a mimeographed underground newspaper—kind of a neighborhood gossip sheet. It referred to gambling and drinking from time to time, but our idea of "underground" then was pretty tame compared to what it is today.

The whole world of journalism appealed to me. I was, for instance, interested in the way city desks and managing editors played stories in the papers, but it was the glamour of reporting which I found most appealing. I thought that being a foreign correspondent would be the ultimate, though I never really expected to attain that goal. In a general way, that has been true of my entire career. I never was goal-oriented in the sense that the phrase usually is used. I just wanted to do a really good job—the best job I could—at whatever I was doing at the time, and from that job I aimed for the next job opportunity I saw. I never had in my mind a clear-cut path to follow through a preplanned succession of jobs to a high position such as managing editor of *The New York Times* or president of CBS News. I've been an opportunist really, always keeping my eye on the next opening and taking it when it came.

In college I didn't do well. I wasn't a good student, because I skipped most of my classes and spent the time working. In my junior year I got a really good, full-time job offer to cover the state capital for the Scripps-Howard news bureau, which serviced three newspapers in the state, and I dropped out of college to take it. I was a cub reporter in a sense, although I was fairly skilled by then, but the job was at a cub's salary. The other two people, who ran the bureau, were a husband-and-wife team, Dick and Eleanor Vaughan. They were excellent journalists and taught me a lot. Then the Houston *Press*, one of the three papers we serviced, offered me a job at $15 a week, and I took it.

After I was with the *Press* about a year, I visited my grandparents in Kansas City on vacation. While there, I discovered that a new radio station had started up. Kansas City seemed like the Big Apple, and I felt that working there would really be getting into the big time. So I applied for a job at the station. I suggested I could be their news editor. It was a very small station, and they said, "Well, you can be our news editor *and* our sports editor." I gave notice to the Houston *Press*, and the station hired me for $25 a week.

The work was interesting, but the station lacked a serious approach to news coverage. We didn't have a news wire. We just read the local newspapers and took from them, and the program director was a former singer who constantly interfered with the news. His wife would call up if she saw a big fire. Because she had seen it, that was the big news of the day, and we had to get it on the air. Maybe that station was particularly ridiculous, but this sort of thing was going on all through radio news in those days, and I wasn't happy with it. So after a year or so I happily got back into newspaper reporting by taking a job with the United Press wire service.

UP sent me right back to Texas. I wasn't there long when Gayle Grubb, manager of radio station WKY in Oklahoma City, called me. He recently had bought the rights to broadcast the University of Oklahoma football games and was looking for an announcer. At a Chicago convention of the National Association of Broadcasters he had heard from August Schlicker, the manager of the Kansas City station, that I was the finest football announcer going. The truth of the matter is that I never had done a live football game. I just had used a Western Union play-by-play sports service and constructed from my imagination what might have been happening on the field and in the stands.

I went to Dallas to audition for the job anyway, and the man from Oklahoma City asked how much money I would want to come to his station. I was planning marriage by then and looking toward getting some money together, so I took my UP salary and tripled it. I never thought he would pay it, but he did, and I quit UP and went to Oklahoma. When the football season was over I moved into the news department for the rest of the year to wait until we got into the next football season. But again I was terribly unhappy in the news department.

WKY probably was one of the best stations in the Southwest, but radio just wasn't the newspaper business, and it was not until World War II that broadcast news gained respectability, thanks to Edward R. Murrow and a lot of others. Broadcasting never seemed to me to be a respectable business in the 1930s. On the local level, at any rate, it was trying to mold something half of entertainment and half of news, with the news very clearly being an adjunct of show business. It lacked the dedication and integrity I felt comfortable with.

I'm disappointed today in the trend away from newspaper training. A lot of people coming into broadcast news straight out of
college are well trained, dedicated, interested, and probably
brighter than we were. They are more roundly educated than most
of us were forty years ago, when a lot of newspaper people had no
formal education. There's no question about that, and these young
people are proving to be very good broadcast journalists, but I think
they would be even better if they had two or three years of newspaper experience. If you were to ask someone straight out of college to
go down and check out a story in the probate court, I bet you
wouldn't find one out of a hundred who would know what you were
talking about. Yet there are a lot of stories in a probate court.
Newspapers know that. They have people in the courts every day,
and they constantly are covering city hall as a beat. Graduates who
go right to work in a local radio or television station never learned
the beat. They're covering four or five stories a day. They get into a
story, five minutes later they're out of it, and then it's fifteen
minutes to get the tape to the station. The coverage is slapdash. It's
much too hasty, much too thoughtless.

During those first three or four years out of school when I was
bouncing between print and broadcasting, it really was a case of
finding myself—experimenting. I'm glad now that I did, because I
think it was all for the better. I had one side excursion into business,
though, due to my dissatisfaction at WKY.

A friend of mine had been doubling as public relations director
and assistant traffic manager at Braniff Airways until he was promoted to something like general traffic manager. It was a major job,
and he persuaded me to become publicity director for the airline. As
it turned out, he didn't have the authority to do that. So when I
showed up at Braniff, that job did not exist. I already had quit WKY
and I wound up at Braniff anyway, doing some public relations
work but mostly running the north end of the airline—handling
sales and everything else. I enjoyed it very much. It was a pioneering
venture—a new airline in a relatively new field—and it was great

fun. I very well might have stayed, but after a year the war in
Europe was beginning to form up. It was about the time of Cham-
berlain's meeting with Hitler in Munich, and it was pretty clear
things were going to get a lot worse before they got better. I couldn't
very well see myself letting a war go by without being in the news
business. So I appealed to UP to let me come back, and they did.

I spent the next eleven years with UP, and as a foreign
correspondent I wound up covering, among other things, the battle
of the North Atlantic, the Allied invasion of North Africa, the
Normandy beachhead assaults, and the Battle of the Bulge. That
was a very formative period—I don't know what would have happened had I been back in the States covering domestic news—and it
flowed over into the postwar period.

After reporting the surrender of Germany I spent a short while
reorganizing the UP bureaus in Brussels and the Netherlands. Then
I covered the war crimes trials at Nuremburg for a year. In 1946 UP
sent me to Moscow, where I spent the next two years as chief
correspondent for the wire service.

In 1948 I returned to the States for a home leave, which coincided
with the birth of our first child. My wife, believing that no child
could properly be brought into the world unless it was in Kansas
City, had flown halfway around the globe from Moscow for the
event. I followed, stopping off in London. After discussions there
with UP, I had every thought of returning as the general European
news manager. It was a job I wanted more than any other. I was
terribly eager for it, and that was my general plan for the future. It
was purely by accident that I wound up instead with CBS.

While in Kansas City I had lunch with a good friend, Karl
Koerper, who was vice-president and general manager of KMBC,
the CBS affiliate in Kansas City. It was a very fine, responsible radio
station—the sixth station Bill Paley had put together of the original
CBS network.

Karl and I were having just a social lunch at the Kansas City Club,
and I noted that the spirit in the Midwest—particularly in Kansas

City, which I knew best—had died in the years I had been gone, during the war years and immediately thereafter. Although he was a big civic leader and on the ladder to becoming the head of the chamber of commerce, Karl conceded that it was possibly so. I said, "You know, I notice the same thing in Des Moines, Omaha, Oklahoma City, Tulsa—all through this corner of the world." The Kansas City *Journal* had since died, and I theorized, "I think it's because of the fact that journalistic competition has lessened; that with the death of the second newspaper something of the spirit of a town disappears." He nodded that I might be right. Then, waxing into my subject, I said, "Furthermore, Karl, I think it's your fault. You guys in radio have cut up the advertising dollar so many ways that only one newspaper can exist, and you haven't done anything to take the place of the newspapers you've thrown out of business." He said, "Now wait a minute. Do you know how many people we have in the newsroom at KMBC?" I said, "No, Karl, I don't." He said, "Eight." I said, "My gosh, Karl, do you know how many people they've got in the city room of the Kansas City *Star?*" He argued, "Oh, wait a minute. That's their principal business." I said, "Thanks. You just answered my whole argument. It's finished. That's their business. It's not yours."

The discussion ended on quite an adversary note, but Karl called a few days later and said, "I've been thinking about what you said. Maybe you're right. I want to have lunch with you again." We did, and he asked, "What would you do about this situation?" I said, "First, I would be sure to cover those places where the principal news directly affecting the citizens of your listening area is made— the county courts, the city hall, the state house—and it's difficult being on the state line, because you have to cover two, but that's the first thing I would do. Then Washington. I'd get right to the real fundamentals of the news which hits the guy at Twelfth and Main Street, and I don't think you're doing it. You're really just relaying what the wire services report."

Later we had another meeting, and Karl asked, "What would you charge to go to Washington for us?" Again I tripled my salary, figuring Karl never would meet it, but he did. So I went to Washington for a group of stations he had put together. I was doing that for about a year and a half when the Korean War broke out, and Ed Murrow asked if I would go to Korea for CBS.

I originally had met Ed during the war in London, where he once before had offered me a job. I actually had accepted that offer but later reneged on it. He felt I had broken a handshake agreement, and he was right. I don't think he ever quite forgave me, and I felt badly about it for a long time. I still do. So it was a surprise when he asked me to go to Korea. This time I accepted in earnest. KMBC let me out of my agreement with them on the condition that I do some coverage for them in Korea and return to them after I finished in Korea for CBS, but that never worked out. I never got to Korea.

I had been with the CBS radio bureau in Washington for only a few weeks—getting my shots and attending the Korea briefings at the Pentagon—when a series of things happened. About two or three people from the bureau had gone to cover the war in Korea, and a couple of others in Washington got sick. It was the middle of the summer, and they couldn't quickly reach the people who were on vacation. So I was asked to do Eric Sevareid's eleven o'clock evening news. I was a neophyte, but I went right on the air doing a fifteen-minute newscast and commentary. It was incredible. It was a major radio network broadcast, but that's how desperate they were. Then CBS suddenly acquired a television station they had applied for in Washington. They never expected it to come along so quickly, but the Federal Communications Commission suddenly said, "Okay, CBS. You can have it."

The station—WTOP, then WOIC—had had a very poor news operation, and CBS asked me to go on the air and do the Korean War story, which was the big story at that time. They simply said, "Go out and do five minutes on the evening news." They asked what I needed, and I said, "Just give me a blackboard with an outline of Korea with the 38th parallel marked on it." I adlibbed it—a chalk talk—which was no big deal, because it seemed I had spent half my life at war briefings. After about three days they said, "How about doing the whole newscast?" I thought I'd be doing it that day, the next, maybe a week, and then be off to Korea. So I said sure and I adlibbed the whole thing. CBS soon sold the newscast— had gotten commercial backing—but it didn't mean anything to me because I was not commercially conscious of what that meant in television broadcasting. Then they asked me to take the eleven o'clock television news also, which meant more dollars for me, and they quickly got sponsors for that too.

So I was doing two fifteen-minute programs a night. After a couple of weeks I asked, "What happened to Korea?" They said, "Your're not going to Korea. You've got two commercial news programs." I fought furiously to keep from becoming a success, because I wanted to go to Korea in the worst way. I was very mad and said, "This isn't what I signed up to do." They told me, "That's not what your contract says. It just says you came to work for CBS." It really was a nasty little fight, but they convinced me I should stay.

I don't know where broadcast news would be today if it hadn't been for Ed Murrow and others—like Elmer Davis, the antithesis of a show business approach with his Indiana voice and raspy delivery. That partly may have been why he appealed to me, but more than anything it was the intensity of such people in the pursuit of journalism—the sense that they cared. It really all goes back to Bill Paley. He saw to it that CBS hired people like Ed Klauber and Paul White who were dedicated to making something out of broadcast news. It was because of them that Murrow was on board, and what he accomplished made it possible for me even to consider going to CBS in the late 1940s.

I don't know why I'm a success—what that "special" quality is. I watch myself on the tapes and think anybody could do a better job, and most of them can. It's silly to say, but maybe we're just made for each other.

Ron Field

Ron Field started in dance for the simple reason that his aunt was a dance teacher in his native New York City. He first appeared on Broadway at a very young age and later went on to appear in other Broadway perform-ances, with stock companies, and on television and in nightclubs. He was dancing with a stock company in Indianapolis when his choreographic ability emerged. For many seasons he was choreographer for Ed Sulli-van's Toast of the Town, *and since then he has choreo-graphed three Broadway shows, including* Cabaret, *and choreographed and directed two others, including* Ap-plause. *He also has choreographed and directed a num-ber of television specials and nightclub acts for such performers as Ann-Margret, Liza Minnelli, Joel Grey, Carol Channing, and Cyd Charisse. He has won two Academy Awards, an Emmy Award, and a TV Critics Circle Award, and is a member of the Entertainment Hall of Fame.*

It's interesting how people wind up where they do. Life doesn't give you the opportunity to raise your hand in the very beginning and take your pick of what you want to be.

My aunt was a dance teacher. As a result, I wound up on the ballet barre and doing tap when I was five or six years old. Some other kid might have said, "I don't want to do this sissy stuff. I want to play ball. Buy me a ball, dad. Buy me some football equipment." I didn't. Dancing was fun, and I took to it naturally, and the more I got to dance, the more I pulled away from the things boys my age normally did.

In the afternoons after school, I took the subway to dance class. The more I didn't hang around the neighborhood, the more uncomfortable it was for me to be there, because the other kids made fun of me. I was puzzled and hurt because they treated me like some strange creature. It's interesting how that little kid dealt with all of that. I became happier and happier when I didn't have to go out and compete on the street with the other kids. It was much nicer for me to ride the subway with my school books, go to dance class, get home in time for dinner, do my homework, and go to bed.

I was only eight or nine years old when my aunt took me to audition for the Broadway musical *Lady in the Dark,* which starred Gertrude Lawrence. I got the part and stayed with the show during its entire run. Then I "retired" professionally until, when I was seventeen, I appeared in the musical *Seventeen,* based on the book by Booth Tarkington. I had had good training, having started at such an early age. Luck was with me too, because I grew to be six feet tall and fairly good-looking. When I entered an audition, I was considered an attractive person for a theatrical company.

I had my eighteenth birthday on the road with *Gentlemen Prefer Blondes* and didn't even go to my high school graduation. I had gone to the High School of Performing Arts while attending the American Ballet School on a scholarship. It was when I was sur-

Ron Field: *That second summer in Indianapolis every-one was saying, "Gee, you're good." They didn't know I was nervous, always hoping it would work, always hop-ing a step would come out well.*

rounded by the other dance and drama students there that it all finally seemed natural to me, and I suddenly felt I belonged.

As earnest as I was about dancing, I never made any serious plans about what I would be doing in ten years. I should have, because there's a time—and at a very young age—when you can't leap high anymore and there are eighteen-year-old chorus dancers who are coming up. I was oblivious to the future. Then it just evolved.

I was doing summer stock in Indianapolis—dancing the lead in *Gentlemen Prefer Blondes*. The choreographer was a local guy who wasn't very good. I told him, "Carol Channing did this, and the girls came in here, and we went there, and this, and that." Suddenly I had choreographed the whole show. It was Agnes De Mille's choreography I was showing them, but the producers of the stock company saw something in me. Whatever it was—interest, vitality— they asked me if I would come back the next year as choreographer.

So I suddenly went from dancer to choreographer—not from ambition, because I wasn't ambitious—but because I had been gifted with an inventive mind which not only retained steps but made tasteful choices. That second summer in Indianapolis everyone was saying, "Gee, you're good." They didn't know I was nervous, always hoping it would work, always hoping a step would come out well. The responsibility was a great burden, and the pressure was unceasing. Because it was unrelenting, I never was able to take a deep breath, step back, calmly appraise my work, and say, "Oh, that is good." My life just seemed to be a constant audition, and it has remained so. You audition for the stars and for agents and for managers. For networks and for sponsors and for critics. For the public and for dancers waiting for you to come up with the next step or the next lift.

As a result of my work in stock I received an offer in 1961 to do an Off-Broadway show. It was *Anything Goes*, and it was such a big success that people were coming from uptown to see it. Then I received an offer to choreograph a Broadway show—*Nowhere to Go but Up*. It flopped, but my work got good notices. I began choreographing nightclub shows for the Latin Quarter in New York City and for other clubs in Miami, Paris, Las Vegas. Then I did my second Broadway show—*Café Crown,* but it flopped too.

One day after I returned from Lebanon, where I had staged a lavishly produced spectacular, my agent said to me, "You've cooled. We've got to put some heat under you. The Off-Broadway show was four years ago, and even though your work was fine, you've been involved with two flops on Broadway. I don't know whether this will work or not, but another client of mine is putting together a night-club act for Liza Minnelli." I said, "Judy Garland's daughter! That's going to make a lot of noise. She's only nineteen, and hardly anyone has seen her, but I hear that she's an extraordinary talent. I'll do that act for nothing." My agent asked if I would be willing to have her interview me first, and I agreed.

When we met, I said, "Look, Liza, you don't know what I'll come up with. Some people talk a great show. Let me pick a song we can do a routine to. It won't necessarily be in the act, but after eight hours we'll know if the chemistry is right between us." Two days later we met again in a rehearsal studio, and after four hours she said, "You're terrific." I was hired. She opened four weeks later in Washington, D.C., and got a standing ovation. Everywhere she played she got rave reviews.

On the strength of that act, Hal Prince hired me to do *Cabaret.* That got me a Tony Award, and I was extremely proud of it, but secretly I still was not at all secure in my own talent. I continued to worry about the next "audition." I didn't believe in myself. I played down my achievements, telling myself they were easy to do. The people I admired all seemed like intellectual, dedicated, and ambitious geniuses who were far above me. When I visited Jack Cole or Jerry Robbins or Agnes De Mille I found their homes filled with books on dance and theater, libraries filled with research. I thought, "I'll never be able to innovate anything that will put me in the index of any theater glossary." I decided, if that was the case, I'd stay with work I could feel relatively comfortable with. I had no interest in reaching for the unreachable star, because it seemed all you did was strain your arm or sprain your shoulder. Besides, if it's unreachable, I thought, why reach for it?

Life has a way of letting you waft through when you're making enough money to be comfortable, but then I hit a bad slump. It lasted for about a year and a half, and for a while I didn't think I ever would get out of it.

I had recently moved from the East to the West Coast, and I wasn't able to get into the swing of things. I accepted a job to do a production number I didn't believe in. It was for an Academy Awards show, and the whole thing didn't make any sense to me, but—just like a kid—I agreed to do it. I said, "Sure. Okay. I'll do it just the way you want." After I saw it on television, I told myself, "Watch it, Ron. You are succumbing, giving in. You are doing things that really are damaging." I got into my car and drove into the California desert for three days. I knew I had to get hold of myself; that if I wasn't careful I would spend the rest of my life sitting by the pool and waiting for the phone to ring.

The turning point came in 1975. Chita Rivera was in rehearsal for the musical *Chicago* when the choreographer, Bob Fosse, had a heart attack, which delayed the Broadway opening for three months. Since neither Chita nor I had anything to do, I suggested that I put a nightclub act together for her. There was no pressure. We were doing it for ourselves. In ten days—instead of weeks and weeks—it was done. I called a friend who owned the Grand Finale, a little club on West 70th Street in Manhattan with a tiny stage and low ceiling. I asked him, "What about Chita?" He said, "We'd love to have her, but we can't pay much." I told him, "This isn't for money. Just give us two weeks." On opening night I looked up, and something happened to me. I said, "Wait a minute. Whoever did that act is really, really talented." I suddenly had a self-awareness and felt secure in my ability.

About the same time Chita opened, I went to see a preview of *A Chorus Line*. Almost everyone in the show had worked for me at one time or another—in *Cabaret*, in *Applause*, in nightclubs. Michael Bennett, who conceived, choreographed, and directed the show, had worked as my assistant on my first Broadway show. I knew them all. By the time the lights went down and *A Chorus Line* started, I was ready to see a good show. It was so good it stunned me. I couldn't breathe. I couldn't laugh. I couldn't applaud. I couldn't do anything. It was as though my life was there on stage. It was about a choreographer and the dancers he was auditioning. I had been a dancer auditioning. I am a choreographer. It really was like my life was there. I was so moved I couldn't even go backstage after the show. The next day I sent a telegram saying, "Every note, every word, every person is unbelievably perfect. I've never been so inspired in my whole life."

But that night I just walked around for hours. A lot of things went through my mind as I walked. Okay, enough fooling around, I thought. Get your nose to the grindstone and concentrate. No more wafting through life. Use it. No more of, "You have real good instincts and sensitivities, but they don't know you're just sliding by." Apply your talents where you feel you should apply them. Be selective. Take chances. Sure, I thought, I may fall on my ass, but if I fall, I'll fall hard.

Until the Chita thing and *A Chorus Line* I continually acted like a kid who was grateful for everything, going around and saying, "What? Sure. I'll do it your way," or "Could you please consider maybe doing the number this way?" I always had been like that, never believing in myself. That all changed in 1975, and it was like a whole new beginning for me. I decided that—now in my forties—I was not going to walk around anymore thinking, "Gee, I'm so lucky." Since then I have said good-bye to some very important people in this business. I no longer feel obliged to say yes to everything. I can't help it if I'm still nervous driving to work, wondering if something good is going to come out of my head that day or if Danny Kaye or Ann-Margret or Bette Midler is going to be happy with it. I can't help that, but accepting who and what I am—which is healthy—I can tell myself, "If you can't come up with it, hardly anyone else can, because your talent is good. So relax."

My principal focus now is to do an important piece of theater, but I don't want to go back to Broadway to do just another musical comedy. I had my *Applause* trip—a big commercial success. Now I want to do something that will be enlightening as well as entertaining. Otherwise, I would rather continue doing television and nightclubs and movies. If you work with good producers on television the product will be good and tasteful, and you can be proud of it. Movies can be good too, but as far as I'm concerned, Broadway is still *it*.

In 1976 a friend suggested a musical comedy, and I told him I wanted to be involved in a show that would say something. I told him, "I don't think anyone has put into an entertainment form the correct, definitive statement on where homosexuality and the gay consciousness have gotten. That's the show I want to do, and I will be very proud if I can make a contribution by helping to overcome the prejudice that exists toward homosexuals."

There are hideous misunderstandings about homosexuality. It represents the second largest minority in America. There are as many as 20 or 25 million homosexuals from coast to coast, but there are still people like Anita Bryant who are saying, "I don't want them to teach my eight-year-old." How hurtful that kind of thinking is. It's almost barbaric. Sure there are a lot of gay people who act foolishly, who act badly, who are disgusting—but what group is without that? For every one of those, there are hundreds of others who just want to live a good life. Think of what homosexuals have gone through. Think of the prejudice. Think of the lack of understanding. I'm lucky. I have a house. I have a pool. I have a Mercedes. And I have a career which my homosexuality does not jeopardize. But most people don't, who if they weren't so scared might have an opportunity to *be*. After all, we have contributed. We have painted ceilings in churches that people look up at and say, "Oh, Michelangelo." We've built buildings people live and work in. We write books people read. We make music people sing and dance to. We manage corporations. We are educators. We even pushed the gun out of the hand of a woman who was going to kill the President in San Francisco.

I am so glad that, if I had to grow up a homosexual—which is out of the norm and a subculture in society—I wasn't a black sheep among white; that I wasn't a coal miner trying to live out my life in hiding.

Roberta Flack

VOCALIST

Born in North Carolina, raised in Virginia, and schooled in Washington, D.C., Roberta Flack trained as a concert pianist. Friends and teachers made it possible for her— although her family was poor—to study piano and attend the school of music at Howard University on a scholarship. When a counselor advised her to take education courses because of the few opportunities for a black concert pianist at that time, she changed her major from piano to music education. She taught for a number of years but kept performing during that time and appeared in several clubs and restaurants in Washington, D.C. Then in 1968 she left teaching to devote herself entirely to a career as a singer. The following year she made her first record and since then has become known worldwide as one of today's leading singers of popular music.

When I was a young piano student one of my teachers said to me one day, "Roberta, you stick with music. It will never let you down, and it will take you places you never would get the chance to go." She was Hazel Harrison, one of the first fully accepted, black concert pianists. I took what she said very seriously, but it frightened me. It was like telling me, "You cannot walk away from this thing."

My music actually evolved as though I had nothing to do with it. It was as if there was something there which had to come out, but it all happened very gradually and very naturally. At each stage in my development I felt, "Here is the light." I followed that light wherever it took me, and then—without my planning it—something else always happened which swept me along. Every time I went into something new, though, I went into it wholeheartedly.

I sometimes think it was fate that someone who was born into such a lowly situation could rise up out of it through music. There are so many people in the world who love, appreciate, enjoy, and participate in music on different levels, but music becomes a special thing for only a few. There are so many Stevie Wonders out there, for instance, that we never have heard from and never will hear from.

For me there always were what I call golden opportunities. I always had music smiling up at me.

My mother was a church organist in Asheville, North Carolina, near where I was born. I remember having temper tantrums whenever she tried to leave me at home. As a result, I got to accompany her to a lot of rehearsals and to sit beside her on the organ stool. I was three, and I made a complete pest of myself by insisting on playing, but I never had the feeling I was doing anything wrong. It just was good, and since my mother was the light of my life it had double meaning for me. In my mind's eye I still can see the church. I still can see the organ and the organ stool, and somewhere in my head I can still hear the particular sound of that organ.

Roberta Flack: *My mother had only gone as far as the tenth grade, and my father had a third-grade education, but they both were very literate. They spoke well, and their values were high. They drummed into our heads that the situation you live in doesn't have to live in you.*

We moved to Arlington, Virginia, when I was four or five. My mother's two sisters lived in the area. They all were domestic workers, but Arlington seemed to offer a more promising way of life than we had in North Carolina. The house in which we lived in North Carolina was a shack with an outhouse, but I wasn't aware of hard times. At that young age everything was beautiful to me.

In Arlington we lived first in the basement of a house in which another family lived upstairs. It had two bedrooms and one larger room with a potbellied stove, which was sort of the center of things. The bathroom there was outdoors too, but the house was a decided improvement even though the space was smaller and we were cramped. We all slept in the two bedrooms—my mother and father, my grandmother, my aunt and two cousins, my three sisters, my brother, and I. After four years we moved up the block into a house which had been a one-family unit but which had been subdivided. There we had one bedroom, a living room, and a tiny kitchen, and we shared a bathroom with another family. My father later built on another room so that we kids had our own bedroom.

Arlington was a typical situation, I suppose, of lower-class black families with a large number of people living in limited space. Although we were poor we were better off than a lot of people, who sometimes didn't have food to eat, and in our own way we were considered snobbish. My mother had gone only as far as the tenth grade, and my father had a third-grade education, but they both were very literate. They spoke well, and their values were high. They drummed into our heads that the situation you live in doesn't have to live in you. My mother went to church all the time, and we all had Sunday clothes. This was in a neighborhood where people were being murdered and there were dope addicts and alcoholism. In the middle of all that I played classical music.

For me, playing the piano was like playing with dolls for other little girls. It was fun. I used to play on a piano we had at Sunday school, and when I was nine the superintendent of the school decided I should take piano lessons. She told my mother and father she would pay for the lessons, and she found a teacher for me. I needed a piano to practice on at home, so my father found one, brought it home, and fixed it up. I used to say he found it in a junkyard. I really don't know where he found it, but it looked like a junkyard piano. If it wasn't, I hate to think of where else it could have been, because it smelled of rat urine constantly. I grew up practicing on that piano.

At age nine I also switched from the elementary school in Arlington to another all-black school in Washington, D.C. My mother made the move for my brother and me because she wanted us to have a better education. My parents always were concerned about our education. As I look back now I recognize subtle things they said and did that provided us with motivation and made a difference in the education we received.

Although I was only nine I already was in the sixth grade when I changed schools. I was very short. The teachers took one look at me and said, "There's no way you can be in the sixth grade." So without giving me an examination or anything they put me back, and I repeated the fifth grade. About six or seven months after I changed schools, Washington introduced a tuition bill to cut down on the number of students who were coming to the District schools from Maryland and Virginia. These mostly were black children. Some were excluded from having to pay the tuition, and—because of my IQ or whatever—I happened to be one of them.

Through elementary school, junior high, and high school I became very secure in my musicianship. I achieved a lot of recognition for my music, but I took it for granted because everyone else did. I was a tiny girl who sat on the piano bench before the whole school during assemblies and played the school song and the national anthem, and I played the accompaniment for the school choirs. Nobody made a big thing of it, which, as I look back now, was quite good, because I believe children can be spoiled in terms of their pursuits if they are constantly applauded—especially in the black community where I grew up; where all of us were poor and had basically the same family situation. To come out of that, because of any little successes, with something different from what everyone else has can make you proud but also uncomfortable. And while you might be proud about what you can do, you can't think about that. You might win scholarships and walk off with a $10 prize here or $20 there, but that money doesn't change the situation in which you live. I got up mornings in the same house, went to school with the same kids, and ate the same food—beans during the week and maybe a piece of chicken on Sundays. That reality always was there. Applause doesn't change that. It was a sense of challenge—the desire to play and be really, really good—that did more for me than flattery ever could have done.

I had an assignment from my first piano teacher when I was ten to play Rachmaninoff's *Prelude in G Minor*. It was very difficult, but I played it with a lot of feeling and only a few mistakes. Had I worked a bit harder and known it a bit better, it would have been great. At any rate, my teacher invited her sister to come downstairs to listen. I found out later the sister was a cruel person, but she just sneered when I finished and said, "She can't do that." I could have cried or stormed out of there, but I didn't. I just took what she said and told myself, "I may not be the best, but I damn sure will be." The next time, I had the piece memorized, and it was perfect.

I graduated from high school at age fifteen with a music scholarship to Howard University as a piano major. That was an especially young age for a person to be going to college from the community where I grew up. Most of my classmates were eighteen, nineteen, and twenty. It was not that I was smarter. Some of the others had become pregnant and dropped out, gotten into trouble and dropped out, had to go to work and dropped out—or whatever. I just did not allow myself to be distracted. I practiced my music five and six hours a day. My only other major interest—unfortunately—was eating, but I had no passion like music. Not playing, not bicycle riding, not learning how to dance, not dating. There wasn't anything else for me. I never made any of those other choices over my music. What diversions I did have were all musical. In high school I loved

Patti Page and Jo Stafford. I wanted to sound like Jo Stafford singing "See the pyramids along the Nile . . ." in four-part harmony. So I formed a girls' quartet, and I had them sounding like her. I was not into voice in a formal way at all, however, except as a member of school choirs, and I joined those only because I was the accompanist—all through junior high and high school.

The scholarship to Howard came about through personal connections. My high school music teacher was the sister of the assistant to the dean of music at Howard—Dean Lawson—and they got me the scholarship to the school. My goal was to become a concert pianist, but at the end of my freshman orientation week I got my first inkling that something else might be on the horizon for me musically.

We had a freshman talent show at the end of that week. I had been working as an accompanist with a couple of girls who were going to sing in the show. One of them was Barbara Graham, a cute little girl from Atlanta, Georgia, who everyone thought would win, but she got sick at the last minute. They asked me to play something in her place on the program. Then the senior in charge of the program, who had heard me sing while coaching Barbara, said, "Roberta, why don't you sing? Practically everyone else is going to play something. We need a singer." I told her, "Oh, no. I can't sing." She said, "Please." I said, "No. I can't do it." But finally I agreed.

June Christie's "Don't Take Your Love from Me" was a big number at that time, which was in the mid-1950s. So I went out and sang it off the top of my head—just the way she would have done it—and won first place. Two of the judges were from the music school, and they chose me reluctantly. The music school was particular about the kind of music you could play or sing, and the judges let me know that. Dean Lawson really made a big thing about it. He called me into his office and said, "We don't want you to do that kind of music. It's very bad for the school." I know now what he meant, but it terrified me to hear him say it. I wanted to be free to develop my music, and my instincts told me there were all sorts of music I should try even though my studies all were classical music.

I was a serious music student at Howard. I made good grades and achieved a little notoriety on the campus as a heavy musician, but I managed to do other things on the side every once in a while. I enjoyed listening to the Four Freshmen, and I formed a quartet which copied their music note for note. Somehow I could pull things out of people. I could talk to them about music in such a way as to make them really sing.

A fraternity at Howard sponsored a songfest each year, and when I was a freshman one of the sororities came to me and said, "We would like you to work with us for the songfest. We want to win, and we heard you can help us." I took one of the university choir pieces and rearranged it. I thoroughly rehearsed the sorority singers, directed them in the songfest, and they won. I still don't believe I did that. They were all juniors and seniors, and I was still a fifteen-year-old kid—a *green* fifteen-year-old kid. I had had no previous experience at all except at my church and with the little junior high and high school things I had done. There wasn't anyone to tell me you conduct from left to right or anything like that. It was all instinct.

In my senior year the incident from freshman week almost repeated itself. Iota Phi Lambda, a civic-oriented sorority, had a contest every year to raise money for scholarships, and they gave prizes—something like $100 for first place, $50 for second, and $25 for third. I decided to compete, because I needed some extra money. I already was teaching piano at two settlement houses in Washington, and I was working with the nurses' choir at Freedmen Hospital, the university hospital. I also directed the senior choir at the church in Arlington. I went there Thursday evenings for rehearsals and then went back on Sundays to play for the church services, but I still found time to get a group together for the sorority contest—a bass player, a drummer, a trombone player, and a background singer. We worked like dogs for three weeks. The audience screamed when we did our number, and we got second place. Based on their reaction, we should have won, and I began seriously to think that maybe something else was happening for me in music. One of the judges, though, was the assistant to Dean Lawson, and he almost didn't let me graduate because I had participated in the show.

From college I went into teaching. Although I had started at Howard as a piano major, I changed my major to music education at the end of my sophomore year. Dean Lawson had called me into his office and said, "If you leave here with a major in piano, that's all you will have. You ought to get some education courses just in case you need them." That made sense to me, because at that time black concert pianists were not enjoying the success others were. The same opportunities weren't there for them, especially if they were dark and had short, nappy hair. So after the conversation with Dean Lawson I agreed that I should prepare myself, and I became a music education major. Besides, I saw it as another kind of challenge.

My first year out of Howard I taught in Farmville, North Carolina. Even while teaching I took advantage of every opportunity I could to perform. There wasn't much opportunity in Farmville, but I did have my class do a classical music concert. I had rehearsals on Tuesdays and Thursdays and got up at six o'clock in the morning to meet them at school by seven. At the end of that year, I decided to come back to Washington. As soon as I got assigned to a school, I did the same thing again with the kids. I formed a singing group of about twelve girls and taught them little routines.

No matter where I was, I always was looking for someplace where I could play, someplace where I could sing, someplace where I could get involved with music of some kind. Somehow it always turned out to be a stepping stone to something else.

One Sunday afternoon at a church service I met a girl named Alberta Driver, who sang at various churches. We were on the same program, and her piano player hadn't shown up. So I sight-read her music and played her accompaniment. Afterward she said, "You've got to come and meet Mr. Wilkerson, my voice teacher." When I went with her to his studio he asked me to play and hired me as a studio accompanist. I worked there afternoons and evenings after school. That was a great challenge and a tremendous growing experience. Whoever came in, it was my job to sight-read their music and accompany them. I got involved with all kinds of music for different kinds of singers. Each form represented a wealth of music, and I kept absorbing it—growing stronger all the time. Within a year I found myself conducting Mr. Wilkerson's students in the entire opera of *Porgy and Bess* and in the last act of *Aïda*. I hadn't even been trying to find a way to get involved with that kind of music, but things like that kept coming to me.

Then I got an opportunity to work at the Tivoli opera restaurant in Georgetown. My piano teacher was an accompanist there, and I filled in as a substitute, accompanying the operatic singers who performed. Soon I was a regular accompanist too, but still teaching and still working in Mr. Wilkerson's studio.

One evening during Christmastime 1967 the Tivoli was really busy. The manager asked me to play in between the performances so that the people wouldn't get restless while waiting for their dinners. I started playing Christmas carols, but that seemed to bore them. I switched to arias, and they liked that, but then I decided to sing. It was a beautiful snowy night, and I sang "The Christmas Song" ("Chestnuts roasting on an open fire. Jack Frost nipping at your nose . . ."). Suddenly the restaurant got extremely quiet, and everybody turned to listen. When I finished they gave me a standing ovation, I think mainly because the people—almost all of whom were regular patrons—were used to me just as an accompanist, but it was perhaps the most thrilling moment of my life as a musician.

The following summer was an important turning point for me. I got jobs playing for a few weeks in each of two clubs in downtown Washington. Then a friend told me that they needed a piano player for Sunday brunch at Mr. Henry's on Capitol Hill. I went in there, auditioned, and the man hired me on the spot. I worked there for the rest of the summer and by September had decided not to go back to teaching.

The whole time I was teaching school I never felt that that was all I was going to do, but neither did I feel that I didn't want to teach, that I had to get out, that it was not my thing. There were a number of things that made teaching a rewarding experience for me. My great joy in teaching was dealing with students who responded and whom I could see developing—coming from nothing and wanting to go on to get master's degrees as musicians or music teachers. As a student teacher, I discovered that you learn a lot by teaching, and in the process I learned so many things. In fact, I think I've gotten as far as I have, not only in terms of professional success but also insofar as my general learning is concerned, because I taught.

After I decided not to go back to the school system that September, I went and talked to George Campbell, the assistant superintendent in charge of secondary education. He said to me, "Roberta, what do you want to do?" I told him, "I want to play, and I want to sing." He was strictly an education person, but he said to me, "Then what are you waiting for? Just go ahead and do it. If that is what you want to do, you don't have to apologize for not teaching. Just go to it."

So I left the school system with no money and kept the job at Mr. Henry's for $20 a week—playing and singing on Sundays from two to six in the afternoon. The following year Les McCann, the jazz pianist, who had just signed a contract with Atlantic Records, convinced them that it would be worthwhile for them to listen to me. They did, and I recorded my first album.

All the feelings I have had from music—all the goosebumps I have received from other musicians and all I feel I have shared—have never been as great as the thrill I am sure I would have enjoyed had I been able to walk out on a stage one night as a concert pianist after twenty-two years of hard practicing. But my interests were in other areas too, so I never have felt any regrets. I developed as a whole musician who enjoys all types of music. Also, had I become a concert pianist I don't believe my life as a performer would have been anywhere near as rewarding as it has been.

Winning Grammy Awards is not what excites me, nor am I

excited by hit records. I am excited by "The First Time Ever I Saw Your Face" because, when I recorded it in 1969, I sang it the way I felt—with no suggestions and no ideas from anybody and with no doubts or insecurities about the way I felt, and it did become a hit and, even more than "Killing Me Softly," made me known worldwide as an artist.

I first got involved with that song when, as a teacher, I did an arrangement of it for a girls' glee club. I started doing it solo when I went to Mr. Henry's, and husbands and wives kissed and made up while I was singing it there. Then I got invitations to sing it at weddings. Everybody reacted to it. When I recorded it for Atlantic I wasn't thinking about a hit. I was thinking only about singing it— singing music that I loved.

Louise Fletcher

ACTRESS

Louise Fletcher, who was born in Birmingham, Alabama, and studied drama at the University of North Carolina, began her professional career as a television actress in California. After an eleven-year break she returned to acting with a minor role in the film Thieves Like Us, *which she accepted more or less as a favor to director Robert Altman. Due to the critical acclaim the film received, she decided to return to a full-time career. She attributes part of the reason for that decision to the women's movement, which encouraged her to feel she could pursue acting while also being a wife and mother. It took more than a year, however, before she was able to find an agent who would represent her. Her second film earned for her an Academy Award as Best Actress of the Year for the role of Nurse Ratched in* One Flew Over the Cuckoo's Nest.

I was in the most trouble I've ever been in in my life the day I went to the movies by myself for the first time. I was eleven, and the picture was *Lady in the Dark* with Ginger Rogers. It had a tremendous impact on me, and I sat through it again and again from the time the theater opened at one o'clock in the afternoon until it closed that night. When I got home I found that my parents had the police out. They were really scared.

The picture had put me in a trance. I never noticed when it started or ended, and it sparked something in me—the thought that I could aspire or dream to be something else, somebody different. It was a portrait of a woman who was one thing—very cold and businesslike—but she had a secret life. In her dreams she was something else. It made me feel that if I put my mind to it I could change the pattern of my life, and I wanted very badly to change it. I wanted a life different from what other girls my age were planning. Southern girls thought the thing to do was what their mothers did: grow up, get married, have children, and stay at home. It was a life without surprises, and I didn't want that. I knew I was not going to do that—that I was going to do something else.

My parents were ambitious for us. They both were totally deaf, and they kept telling us—my brother, my two younger sisters, and me—that we had all the advantages, all our faculties, and that we could become whatever we wanted to be. I believed them. I bought it, and I still believe people can do whatever they really want to do.

I had minor skirmishes with wanting to be a doctor. I wanted to be a concert pianist. I wanted to be a professional tennis player. Mostly pushy, showy things—but they were more fantasies than real ambitions. From the time I was very young, maybe five or six, I thought a lot about being an actress. I didn't tell my friends about my ambitions, though, especially when I got older, because I thought they would not receive them well. I never talked about what I wanted to do. It was like my secret life, and when my friends

Louise Fletcher: The women's movement had had a big effect on me—not in any sort of active way, because I wasn't carrying placards or anything, but the articles I read and the interviews I heard had a definite effect on me. I came to accept that it would be okay to do something for myself.

spoke of their plans to get married and raise their families I talked under my breath. I would say to myself, "Well, I'm not going to do that."

In high school I became very active in drama, clarified my ambitions, and went on to major in drama at the University of North Carolina. Acting came fairly naturally to me. Dinnertime at home was a complete show. To explain to our parents what the day had been like, we would act it out. It was, "Guess what happened to me today? I was sitting on the bus, and this old lady was sitting next to me, and . . ." And you would be the old lady, and you would be yourself. We did that every night. I got a lot from my mother too. Even though she's extremely shy, she's an incredible mimic and can imitate anybody physically. She'd walk the way other people walked and get terrific laughs.

It was my Aunt Beezie who really started my interest in acting. She was a flamboyant character. She lived in Bryan, Texas, and took care of us four kids at different intervals in our lives. I lived with her for a year once and visited her every summer. She had no children of her own, so she treated us like dolls. She gave us singing lessons and piano lessons and dressed us up, and she taught us to show off. She and my uncle were very sociable and would have a lot of people over at night to play cards or whatever. The high spot of those evenings was when we kids got dressed up to do a skit or something to amuse the guests. I loved it.

My father was a minister, and, since several of us went to college at the same time, he couldn't pay for us all. So I had a scholarship from the Episcopal Diocese of Alabama. Twice a year I had to go and see the bishop to report on how I was doing at school and to get my check for the next semester. He was an incredibly handsome, six-foot five-inch man with a great shock of white hair. He had been a wrestler at college and was enormous. He was what I imagined God to be, and after our talks—when I got up to say good-bye—he would put his arms around me. It was like God embracing me, and he would say in his deep, vibrant voice, "Remember who you are and what you represent." I thought I was the only person he ever said that to, until I visited his grave in Alabama in 1976. There on his stone was *Remember who you are and what you represent.* He said it to everybody. But he had the ability of making you feel you were the only person in the whole world he even thought of saying it to, and I've never forgotten it.

The day I graduated in 1957 I left for California with two roommates from college. One of them had a car, and the trip was my graduation present—my expenses and a couple of hundred dollars. I really would rather have gone to New York, since all my training had been in theater, but I didn't have the guts to go there alone. I knew only one person in New York, and that was a man. What I needed was a woman. That's the way Southern girls thought. So I went to California because I had two girl friends to go with. It was easier. My interest in acting was overwhelming, but I wasn't thinking, "I'm going to California and I'm going to become a movie star." Things were different then. I lived just for the moment, and whatever happened, happened. Somewhere in the back of my mind, though, was the ambition to get to New York.

I had very lucky breaks in the beginning. Looking back, I know I made them happen by seeking out certain things. When we arrived in California I started going to acting classes and got a job during the day as receptionist for a pediatrician in Beverly Hills. One day Lee Phillips, who had just been a big smash in the movie version of *Peyton Place*, came in with his kids, and I asked him, "What are you doing now?" He said, "I'm doing a *Playhouse 90* on CBS." I thought, "Oh my God. Such a dream." It must have showed on my face, because he asked if I would like to be an extra in it. "I'd love it," I told him.

The next day he called and told me to be at CBS at a certain time to meet John Frankenheimer, who was directing the show. Besides giving me the job, when he heard I didn't have an agent Frankenheimer called MCA, and they gave me an appointment as a favor to him. I did a scene in their basement theater from something I was working on in acting class, and they signed me. They began submitting me for roles, and I started to work pretty steadily in television. I quit my job in the doctor's office, and as interest grew I began to get bigger and better parts.

Live television drama was like theater, because you moved without thinking about the camera. It followed you around. In film you have to be more aware of what the camera is doing. One of the first shows I did on film, rather than on videotape or live, was an Alfred Hitchcock presentation. The director, Norman Lloyd, said, "Well, you know all about film." I said, "Sure." I played Barry Sullivan's secretary and had a scene where I came into his office, heard a gunshot, screamed, turned, and ran out. After the master shot they changed the setup for a closeup on Barry Sullivan, but I didn't notice they had rearranged the camera, lights, and everything. Norman Lloyd said, "Okay. Do the same thing as you did before." So I came into the office, there was the gunshot, and I screamed, turned, and ran out—knocking down lights, flags, people. I was so embarrassed and humiliated that I could feel the heat in my face, and I kept going. I ran into my dressing room and started to cry. Barry Sullivan came in and said, "What do you care what they think? They don't have to scream and run. Don't be embarrassed." I made it a point after that to check out where everything was. You learn awfully fast when you go through an experience like that.

One of my first starring roles was in *The Lawman* series with John Russell. That was about 1960. It was quite a showy piece, and based on it Warner Brothers offered me a seven-year contract, which I turned down. They were furious and so were my agents, but I felt it was the right thing to do. It was supposed to be for television and film, but Warner Brothers was doing little but television in those days. To me it just seemed they wanted an actress to run from one show to another. It all boiled down to cheap labor. They wanted to pay me $700 a week, instead of the $1,000 I had been getting, for however many weeks a year were involved. Some people argued that the studio would have given me a lot of publicity and that I would have gotten a break in a movie, but the movies they were making then were on the order of *Ice Palace*.

I kept working in television, and then I tested for the picture *Where the Boys Are* and got the part. That was going to be my big break. Before the film started I got married and went on a honeymoon to Mexico City. While we were away Paula Prentiss appeared from out of a cloud. She was sort of zany, and they preferred her personality to mine. I was not zany—which is not to put her down at all, for she was perfect for the part—and when I got back from the honeymoon they had given the part to her. I was terribly discouraged but kept working until 1962 when, on my last job, I was five months pregnant. After our son Andrew was born I wasn't interested in television anymore. It wasn't that rewarding, and I didn't work for the next eleven years.

When we married, my husband—Jerry Bick—was a literary agent, but he sold his business in 1966 because he wanted to become a film producer. The next year we moved to England, where he had a film to do, and we stayed there for six years. While we were there he kept saying, "All these English actresses are playing American women on the screen. It's ridiculous. You ought to do it." But I had totally given up the idea of acting. Once in a while I'd see a film with a really good part and think, "Oh, boy. I could do that," but I would forget it by the time I left the theater.

About 1971 Jerry was working on a film Robert Altman was to direct—*Thieves Like Us*—and Altman said he wanted me to play one of the parts. I joked about it. "You've got to be kidding," I told him. "Not only am I not going to do it, but it's an insult for you to think of me as that woman. She's fifty at least." It was an important film for Jerry, and that was another reason I didn't want to be in it. I didn't want the responsibility. Plus, I was the producer's wife, with all that means. There were just too many things going against it, in addition to the fact that I really wasn't interested. The movie finally got off the ground two years after Altman first offered me the role. We wound up on location in Mississippi, and they still hadn't cast the part. Altman said to me, "You're going to do it." I said, "No, I'm not," but when it came time to shoot they still were counting on me. So I said, "Okay. I'll do it."

I should have been scared after being away from acting for so long, but I was preoccupied with a lot of other things. I was a housewife taking care of two sons. I had reverted to type. I also knew I could handle the part. It was a Southern woman aching for a respectability she never was going to get, and I had known so many people like that. Altman was a big help too. He was marvelous. Once he casts you, you feel there's nobody else who can do the part the way you can. He has the gift of making you feel you're unique for it. Because of the kind of role it was, I could look awful. I didn't have to look good, and looking good can be a big worry. There was not the hassle of getting made up—going through the Hollywood routine of two hours with people poking at your face and your hair so that by the time you get to the actual shooting you're terrified. I just got out of bed in the morning, went to work, and played the part.

Thieves Like Us was not a big money-maker but it was a critical success, and it was a major turning point for me. When I saw it I thought, "That's not bad. I can do that again." I felt very positive and decided that when we got back to California I'd return to work. But it wasn't so easy to do. It took me more than a year to get an agent. I didn't want to draw on any favors, so I contacted only those agents I didn't know. Their responses were incredible: "Why do you want to work? Your husband makes a good living." "I have a lot of middle-aged women who can't get work." Awful things like that.

During the eleven-year period when I had psyched myself up to be a mother and housewife, I tended not to be able to do two things at once. After *Thieves Like Us*, though, I came to believe that I could work and do those other things at the same time. It was difficult, but the women's movement had had a big effect on me— not in any sort of active way, because I wasn't carrying placards or anything, but the articles I read and the interviews I heard had a definite effect on me. I came to accept that it would be okay for me to do something for myself. In fact, during the time I was looking for an agent it was the period of Watergate, and that inspired me to consider trying something really different. I felt I wanted to help change things, and I was thinking, "Why are you doing this to yourself? You're not too old to go to law school."

Finally I went to see an agent I had had at MCA, Wally Hiller. He was very kind and took me on as a favor. It was just coincidental that a week later I got my first interview for *Cuckoo's Nest*. Milos Foreman, the director, had seen *Thieves Like Us* and called me. The first interview was just a casual meeting with Milos. We talked for an hour about Europe, about what I had been doing, about mutual friends. It was very pleasant, and I left. The next meeting was with the producer, Michael Douglas, and the executive producer, Saul Zaentz. It was another sitting-around-talking meeting. Then I got a call to see Milos again and read for him. At this point I was feeling, "Jesus. They're really interested," but I also was hearing all sorts of rumors, such as that Lee Grant had already gotten the part. When I met with Milos we read through a few scenes together. Afterward he said, "Take these two scenes. Learn them and come back at five o'clock."

I had two or three hours, and when I got back Michael and Saul were there too. They obviously weren't convinced and wanted to see me do it. I did the scenes, with Milos playing all the parts except mine. We would do it one way, and—probably to see if I could take direction—he'd say, "No. Let's try it this way." When I got home that evening I thought, "Oh, God. I was terrible. Just terrible." It was December 1975. Jerry had a film to do in Vancouver, and we left for Canada the next day. We were there about two weeks when, the day after Christmas, the phone rang. It was Wally Hiller. He said, "What's a nice lady like you doing playing an awful nurse like that?" I threw the phone down and ran screaming through the apartment. My kids thought I had lost my mind. When I came back and picked the phone up I asked, "How much do they want?" We started filming on January 4 in Oregon.

I feel really, really lucky to have had the eleven-year break away from acting—not to have had more success in those early days. Hollywood can keep you from growing up, and being an actress allows you to be immature if you want to be—especially in dealing with other people. I saw myself in 1977 in a television repeat of a *Perry Mason* show I did in the early days. I was a cute little thing with big eyes and still had a trace of a Southern accent, but there was nothing there. I was like something that hadn't been finished. I wasn't even a person. The years of living abroad and growing up in other ways—not in the Hollywood world—helped.

We all have potentials in us that we don't develop. I'm sure I have potentials in me now that are not developed; that I could and should be developing. People tell me that I've arrived, but I don't feel that way. Maybe it's just that you always want to keep doing things better and better.

David Hume Kennerly

PHOTOGRAPHER

In August 1974, David Kennerly, at age twenty-seven, became the first appointee of the new Ford Administration—as personal photographer to the President. The third and youngest man to hold this White House post, he received a Pulitzer Prize for Feature Photography in 1972 for his work the previous year in Vietnam and India. He won two first prizes in the World Photo Contest in 1976 and has received more than a dozen national and regional awards for his press photography. David Kennerly was born in Roseburg, Oregon, in 1947 and did his first camera work as a school photographer while a junior in high school. As a newspaper, wire service, and magazine photographer, he has covered assignments in almost sixty countries in Asia, Africa, and Europe.

When I was a high school sophomore in Roseburg, Oregon, the photographer for the school paper was sick one day when he was to cover a baseball game. The faculty adviser for the paper showed me how to set the camera, shoved it in my hand, and told me to cover the game. When I saw my pictures in the paper, something snapped. Until then I had wanted to be a veterinarian, but photography rapidly overtook that interest, and I went on to take more pictures for the paper. In the middle of my junior year my family moved to West Linn, a suburb of Portland. Even in high school, photography is very competitive, because there usually is only one slot. They already had someone in it at West Linn, but I soon deposed him even though I had little experience. By my senior year I was taking all the pictures for the paper and for the yearbook. I also had begun to sell pictures at $1.50 each to two small local newspapers, the Lake Oswego *Review* and the Oregon City *Enterprise*. Every now and then I'd get lucky with pictures of a fire or something which the *Oregonian* or the *Oregon Journal* bought.

It was getting more and more exciting for me. It was a whole combination of things: seeing my pictures in the paper with my name under them, knowing what I had to go through to get them, and the challenge of competing with other people to get better ones than they did. I owned a small Rolliflex, but I soon got to the point where I needed a 35-mm. camera. My girl's father was an amateur photographer. He had some nice equipment he let me use, but he warned, "You'll have to be very careful." I said, "Oh, I will. I will."

When you're starting out in newspaper photography you really are an ambulance chaser. That's where you get your dramatic pictures. One day in my senior year there was a big brush fire near my home. I tore out there and was wading through the flames with smoke and ashes blowing all over when I heard over my shoulder, "KENNERLY! My camera!" I looked around, and there was my girl's father. He was a volunteer fireman. He just about had a heart

David Hume Kennerly: I had a working scholarship to Portland State College—Portland State University now. I was to do all the college photography and get my tuition free. But I soon got edgy. I felt school was holding me back, and I had so much energy that I couldn't wait. I just had to go for it.

attack. So did I. I decided I had better get my own equipment. So after I graduated I worked the whole summer in a flour mill—twelve hours a day, six days a week—sweeping floors and loading boxcars with huge sacks of flour. I saved all my money, and that fall I bought my own gear. By then there was no question in my mind about what I wanted to do.

I had a working scholarship to Portland State College—Portland State University now. I was to do all the college photography and get my tuition free. But I soon got edgy. I felt school was holding me back, and I had so much energy that I couldn't wait. I just had to go for it. So before the end of my freshman year, I dropped out of school. I was working part time for a local outfit that put out shopper-type newspapers for five different areas. I didn't like the way they were handling pictures, so I quit. I had heard of an opening on the *Oregon Journal.* There I was, just eighteen with no real experience and applying for a staff photographer's job on the largest evening newspaper in the state. I distinctly remember going out and buying a new corduroy jacket because I wanted to impress them. I went to the assistant managing editor with my pictures from high school and the ones I had gotten into the newspapers. He must have liked my attitude, because I absolutely didn't have the experience needed, but he hired me anyhow.

I had a lot of self-confidence, but I really was winging it, hoping I wouldn't mess up. I knew the basics of what I was doing, but there was a big gap. I talked to people and watched how others handled it. I also was running around like a maniac, covering everything. One time I was leaving the paper about midnight when I heard on the police radio about a big riot—one of the first racial riots in Portland. I jumped into a staff car and went screaming down there. A police car pulled up nearby, and they started to make arrests. Rocks were coming from every direction. Guys were swarming all over, and I was sitting there shooting pictures through the windows of the car. Meanwhile the paper kept calling me on the radio, telling me, "You've got to get out of there. All the other newspeople are staying out." I figured, "Great. We're going to have the only pictures." Then my car started bouncing up and down, and some rioters began to climb on it. I decided it was time to leave. I floored it, and the ones on the back just slid off. Then I looked in the rearview mirror and saw two feet hanging down. A guy up there was hanging on for dear life. I hit the brakes, he bounced off the hood, and the last I saw of him he was racing down the street looking back over his shoulder. That was one of my best stories for the *Journal* before I went off on a six-month tour of active duty with the Army National Guard.

When I got back to Oregon, the *Oregonian* offered me a job. It was a bigger paper and had better photo pages, so I took it. The other photographers were very helpful, David Falconer in particular. He was totally unselfish, a very secure person, and he gave me a lot of advice without feeling threatened. This competitive thing can get pretty sharp. There was one time when a forest fire was raging in the eastern part of the state, and everybody from Portland had flown out to cover it. Twenty fire fighters were trapped for hours on a mountaintop encircled by flames. Our competitors didn't see us and figured they were finally going to scoop the *Oregonian*. When the trapped men finally broke free and reached the bottom of the mountain, Lev Richards—a staff writer for the *Oregonian*—and I were with them. We smiled and waved at the other cameramen, climbed into our plane, and flew back to Portland. We had climbed the mountain when we heard that the men were having such a tough time of it up there. It was touch and go for a while—lots of smoke and hard to breathe—and we barely managed to reach them. But we got an exclusive story. The wire services picked it up, and *Life* almost did a cover.

Shortly after that, on my twentieth birthday, United Press International offered me a job in Los Angeles. I spent a year and a half there and got a solid base of experience covering spot news, professional sports, and every conceivable type of story. I also learned a lot about how much more this business involves than just taking pictures. It's drive. It's enthusiasm. It's diplomacy. It's cunning—that more than anything. Once, an SAS plane went down in Santa Monica harbor. I got down there and looked for a boat. There was only one, a pleasure craft like a houseboat. The Associated Press photographer was coming right behind me, and I asked the skipper, "How much to take me out to the crash?" He said, "I get $700 a day." The AP photographer was getting closer, so I said, "Okay. Let's go." The office almost came unglued when I told them about the $700, but we beat the hell out of AP on that story. Talk about the things you have to do in this business! You get to the scene of a fire after it's out? Start looking for someone with a camera and buy the film. You'd better come back with something, whether it's yours or someone else's.

Later, in 1968, I moved to New York with UPI and spent about nine months there. Larry DeSantis, the UPI picture editor, had more to do with putting my whole act together than anybody. I was ten feet tall when I came walking into the New York bureau. Larry put the brakes on me. He hammered me down to two feet and then slowly let me back up to my normal six. I hated his guts at first, but he was a tremendous help to me in sharpening my skills as a photographer. He'd look at some of my pictures, throw the negatives at me, and say, "This is awful. Go back and do it again." He would get me so damn mad I'd go out fuming—thinking, "I'm going to show him." A lot of people might have broken under the same treatment and figured it wasn't worth it, but I hung in there.

The next stop was UPI in Washington. I had been hesitant to take the assignment. It didn't appeal to me. For one thing, a new man usually had to spend five years or more in the Washington bureau before getting to cover the White House. I thought, "Why go to Washington and not get to do that?" There's one philosophy that has always prevailed through my career: if you want me to work for you, you have to let me do it my way. So I told them in New York that I would go only if I could get on the White House rotation list. It was for a month at a time in rotation with the other bureau photographers. The New York office forced George Gaylin, the bureau chief, to put me on the list. He resented it, and I didn't blame him. He was afraid that I was just going to be a prima donna. I am in a sense, but I've always worked for the overall good of whatever outfit I've been with. That's the only way to go. I believe that a professional in anything is one who doesn't take all the good stuff for himself but works with the rest of the people to produce the best product. But that also means that everybody gets a crack at doing the job. As it turned out, George and I became the best of friends.

Washington finally got to me, though. It had nothing to do with politics. I just found it visually dull. It didn't excite me the way you have to be excited about your work in this business. So in March 1971 I asked to be sent to Vietnam. I felt strongly that I had to do it. I honestly believed—and I believe it more strongly now—that the photographers who are making it in the news end of the business today are the ones who got to Vietnam. A war is the ultimate challenge for a photographer, visually and physically. It runs you through the whole range of human emotions, both in what you photograph and in what you experience. People think, "Oh, the thrilling, glamorous life of a war photographer." But you're covered with mud, you're scared, and you don't know if you're going to get killed or not—which you very well might. That's not glamorous. It's everything that's wrong. I kept myself going by taking pictures. It was when I put the camera down that I thought about where I was, and I was scared.

I was in Vietnam about a year and a half and was bureau chief for Southeast Asia when *Life* made me an offer. I always had dreamed of working for *Life*. My greatest inspirations when I was a senior in high school were two *Life* photographers: Larry Burroughs, who was killed in Vietnam shortly after I got there, and John Dominis, who later became picture editor at *People* magazine. Burroughs had done a memorable story in 1965, "Yankee Poppa 13," about a helicopter crew in Vietnam. Burroughs was on the chopper with them when they got shot up and one crewman was killed. It was a cover—a major picture story with fifteen pages inside. I was deeply moved by it. It wasn't just his war coverage, though. He did other assignments around Asia—all of them brilliant. John Dominis had a series on the big cats in Africa at about the same time, and they were fantastic pictures. Burroughs and Dominis provided me with a sense of direction as to where I wanted to go in the field.

I turned out to be the last contract photographer *Life* hired. The magazine folded about two months later, but even if I had known what was coming I still would have done it. I stayed on with *Time*, first in Vietnam, later in Hong Kong, and then—based in Bangkok—covering Asia. Then to Paris and, based there, spending most of my time covering the war in Mozambique until they moved me back to Washington.

When I had left Washington I felt it was the right move. This time I felt just as strongly that I should be back there. Instinct always has played a key role in my life. In Vietnam it saved my life. I was going up a road and told the driver, "Stop. I don't want to go any further." He turned the car around, and the next car up was ambushed. It's an uncanny thing. After I joined the White House in 1974, we were in San Francisco and before President Ford came out of the hotel there—two minutes before he came out—I told the Secret Service, "You can't let him go over to that crowd. There's something wrong." I had never said anything about anything to the Secret Service before. The head agent radioed up and said, "Be sure to get the President in the car right away." They already had a bad feeling because there had just been a demonstration. All I did was reinforce what they had been thinking. But when I looked at that crowd I had a cold feeling, the same feeling I had had in Vietnam when I was going up that road in the car. So the President came out, and that woman took a shot at him. It went right between me and one of the Secret Service men.

The experience with *Time* was very good for me. John Durniak, the picture editor, had a lot to do with it. He is another man who has been extremely important to my career. If he hadn't trusted and believed in me there's a whole lot of stuff I never could have done. There was the time word was out that Henry Kissinger was going to go to Acapulco on vacation and that he was going to get married before he went. Forever there were rumors that he was going to get married, but John checked it out. He got hold of the editor covering the diplomatic corps, the chief State Department guy who knew Kissinger well, and all the Washington editors. Then he called me and said, "Every source I've checked says that he's not going to get married. It's absolutely not going to happen." I told him, "John, I've covered that guy before. I think he is going to get married. I really do. I have no reason to know for sure, but I feel it. I know it. I better get down to Acapulco right now." He said, "Go."

I was in Dallas–Fort Worth changing planes for Acapulco, and I got paged. It was Durniak: "Kennerly, he just got married, and he's on his way to Acapulco." My plane arrived just before Kissinger's private jet did. I got through customs as fast as I could and was running across the field just as his car pulled out and headed up into the hills. It was a Friday night, and I was the only guy there. It was incredibly frustrating. We could have made that issue of the magazine, but that part of it turned out to be a lost cause.

The Kissingers were secluded at Las Brisas, and more photographers began to arrive, coming from all over the place. Finally everybody was there. There were so damn many people that every time Henry and Nancy went out the gate in their car there were all these photographers in caravans chasing them from one place to another. It was very funny, a real Mack Sennett comedy. Finally Kissinger decided, "All right. If everyone will agree to leave us alone, we'll do a thing." It was Monday afternoon. He and Nancy came out of the foreign minister's house and posed for pictures. I was there and so was everybody else. My stuff went to New York, but I wasn't happy with what I got, and everybody else had the same stuff anyhow. I decided to stay around.

Durniak called me back on Thursday morning. "Dave," he said, "we're going to run a page of color, but the pictures really are mediocre. You've got to try to get something else." I thought, "Oh, my God. I can't get near him." I called up Kissinger's aide, Jerry Bremer, who was down there with him. I said, "Jerry, tell the Secretary that we got this color layout and Mrs. Kissinger doesn't look good at all. Could I come up for five minutes and do a couple of portraits?" He said he would call me back. By now, it was around noon, and the last plane was leaving at four o'clock. Finally they got back to me and said, "Okay. Come on up."

I got there and started shooting like crazy. It was beautiful. The light. Flowers in the background. Beautiful colors. And it was all exclusive stuff of them in their villa. I got the pictures and took off for the airport with a driver going like crazy. I *just* missed the last plane, and there wasn't another scheduled flight to anywhere. I had thought that if I could make it to Mexico City or some place, I could catch a flight to New York, but it wasn't in the cards. By then I was ready to hijack a Mexican airliner if I had to in order to get those pictures to New York. It's not a business where you can just throw up your hands and say, "Well, the last flight left. That's it."

There was a flight—a 707 some company had chartered for a vacation trip. They were flying to Kansas City, but they were full. I said to them, "God, I'll give you anything. I've got to get on that plane." They absolutely couldn't take anyone else. It now was getting on to five or six o'clock. So with nothing else left to do, I stowed away. After everybody boarded, I walked on and went back into the john. The plane took off, and I came out, hanging around and chatting with folks in the aisle because there weren't any seats. They were all IBM types, straight as hell, and there I was wearing a bush jacket. But nobody paid any attention. The passengers didn't care. They were on vacation and in a good mood, and the crew never figured it out.

We got to Kansas City at about one o'clock in the morning, and there were no flights anywhere until a six o'clock flight to Chicago. I sat up all night, got to Chicago, and caught a plane to New York. It was then Friday morning. The deadline had passed for color pictures, but there was still a chance. We landed in New York—it was going on ten—and I practically was beating the cab driver over the head to get through the traffic to the Time-Life Building. When we arrived, I raced up to the color lab, and they started processing the film. Durniak kept calling me. By noon he was yelling, "Dave, you have to get up here. The editors are about ready to go to lunch. You have to get up here now." So I ran down the hall with a carousel tray—still with the same clothes on—throwing bad exposures over my shoulder, leaving a trail of slides behind me. I rushed in as the editors were going out, and they're a tough bunch. I said, "Here. You have to look at this." "Oh, Christ," one of them said, "we've got to go." "Just this one," I said. We projected it—and it was stunning. The most beautiful portrait of Nancy Kissinger you've ever seen in your life. One editor had been chomping on his cigar, but now his mouth hung open. "I want to see more," he said. They wound up tearing out all the pictures in the other layout. Had it been the day before, we would have had a cover. As it was, it cost a lot of bread, but it was worth it—and it wouldn't have happened if Durniak hadn't backed me up.

Another time Durniak supported me was when Gerald Ford became Vice-President. When I first returned to Washington I covered Agnew for two months until his resignation. When Mr. Ford was designated to replace him I said, "John, we've got to cover him full time." Shortly after he was sworn in as Vice-President I made a $100 bet that he would be President of the United States by July. I lost by only one month. I was convinced that he was going to be President.

I was the only photographer who covered Mr. Ford all through his vice-presidency. John, meanwhile, kept saying, "Why do we have to go through all this, all the travel costs and everything? We hardly get any of those pictures in the magazine." I said, "John, let's do it," and he went to the wall for me. During that period I got to know the Fords real well and suggested to them that we ought to have their family album pictures available just in case we needed them. I collected everything—all the good historical stuff: him as a kid, with his mother and father, and so on. I took it over to *Time*, copied it all, and kept the originals until after he became President. We had the only pictures when the time came. The President Ford issue had the cover and twenty pictures inside. All exclusive. *Newsweek* was totaled.

The day after he was sworn in, President Ford called me at the *Time* bureau in Washington. I was sitting in the mail room with my feet on the desk. The switchboard operator nervously informed me that the President himself was on the line. "Hello, Mr. President," I said. "David," he asked, "how would you like a new job?" I was ecstatic. "Sure. When do I start?" "How soon can you be over here?" Ten minutes later I was the official photographer to the President of the United States.

My biggest problem at the White House was keeping myself jacked up professionally, keeping myself sharp, because I was not competing with other photographers. The nature of the position didn't allow it. That's why it would have been difficult for me to stay on for another term of a full four years—although my relationship with the Ford family was and still is very important to me. I think a person should keep broadening himself, setting new challenges.

At noon on January 20, 1977, the moment President Carter took his oath of office, I once again became a freelance photographer. I smiled when, from the Inauguration stand in front of the Capitol, I looked at all the other photographers. I was competing again. I loved it!

Stanley Kramer

PROUDUCER/DIRECTOR

Stanley Kramer, who was born in New York City and arrived on the Hollywood scene in 1933, has produced or directed thirty-five films—the most recent being Raise the Titanic *(1978). In the early years he served his apprenticeship in every kind of studio department. Four stars—Katharine Hepburn, Gary Cooper, Jose Ferrer, and Maximilian Schell—have won Oscars for performances in his films, and* High Noon *alone won four Oscars.* Variety *lists seven of his films as "All-Time Box Office Champions." Kramer includes among his many awards the Irving Thalberg Award, presented by the Academy of Motion Picture Arts and Sciences for "consistent high quality of production." Regarded as one of the most controversial of film makers, he heads his own independent company, Stanley Kramer Productions.*

I went to high school in Hell's Kitchen in Manhattan, and I don't think anyone came out of that unscathed. What the markings are and what causes influences, it seems to me, always are oversimplified and romanticized, but it was tough. Most of the kids seemed to become hoods, prizefighters, or priests. They probably didn't, but they seemed to. There were a lot of mixed races and a lot of high feelings. The feelings, however, seemed to be based more on religious differences than upon race. All the prejudices I saw grew out of that—everything from "Who killed Christ" to a strong Jewish sectarianism—at least among the parents, and the kids grew up adhering to the same narrow views. I rebelled against that sort of thing early, and it turned me from formal religion.

My own thoughts and feelings come from those roots. Without being too emotional about it, I do have a lot of faith when I get up in the morning and see the sun rise, or when I see it set in the evening. I realize there is a tremendous power beyond that which I can comprehend, and I believe that it is not accidental; that somehow there is a direction to things. I'm stunned every once in a while, though, by things which happen in the world, especially man's inhumanity to man.

Some of my distant relatives had been in the distribution end of the film business, and all through my high school years my mother worked as secretary to the man in charge of publicity at the Paramount Theater. I would have to consult a neighborhood psychologist to see if all this had any subconscious influence on me.

In those days it was a five-and-a-half-day workweek. My mother was a widow and I was an only child, and I met her every Saturday at noon. We had lunch at Schrafft's and then went to see whatever movie was playing at the Paramount, for which she had passes.

From the very beginning I was to be "my son the lawyer," but my mind never was on law. In my senior year in high school I won a "Biggest News of the Week" contest that the now long defunct New

Stanley Kramer: *The money was good, but I was terribly unhappy. I had been in all the movie departments— casting, cutting, research, story, property—and I had a feel for film making. I wanted to be a director, but I couldn't even get back into the studios.*

York *World* sponsored for all high school students. I still remember the opening line of my essay. It read, "Last Tuesday, with a 250,000-vote-plurality smile which bade fair to rival his famous welcoming affability, Mayor Jimmy Walker took office for the next four years." That has to be the most impossible sentence in the English language. My prize was $20 and an interview in the newspaper. The reporter asked me what I wanted to be, and I said, "An international banker." If anyone can bridge from there or descend from there to where I am, I'll eat his hat.

After high school I went to New York University, where I took business courses, but I really didn't know what I wanted to do. That education coincided with the Depression, and I developed a great admiration for Franklin Roosevelt when he took over the presidency. I still have a picture of him in my office after all these years. In my opinion, he saved the democracy into which I grew, and he saved it over his enemies, who were 98 percent of the press and certainly all of business. The bugaboo of socialism and communism was running so rampant that the Establishment assaulted every piece of social change on that basis. Even Social Security was thought to be anathema to the free way of life.

When Roosevelt closed the banks he provided hope and put the country on the road back from what was really revolution—the Bonus Army marching on Washington, men selling apples on every street corner of every city, breadlines extending for miles during the middle of winter, the stock market crash, the run on the banks, the whole dislocation. That was real assault on the democratic system, and he saved it.

That all probably had as profound an influence on me as anything on which I can base the things I believe in: my attitudes regarding the situation of blacks, what would happen if atomic war took place and why it shouldn't, the freedom of the teacher to teach in the school, world guilt, sectarian prejudice. I never became any kind of evangelist because of those beliefs, but I later did try to translate the drama of them into film.

When I graduated from NYU in 1933, Twentieth Century–Fox brought me to California at age nineteen to work as a junior script-writer for $60 a week. It was part of a program under which the studio selected graduates who had edited or written for college newspapers and magazines. They took one from each of five colleges, and they chose me from NYU, where I had written some articles for the university magazine. It was just a publicity gimmick, but nobody knew that. The five of us didn't find out until they threw us out after three months. Nobody ever read what we had written in Hollywood, and, even if they had, it couldn't have been anything but drivel.

My mother followed me to California to set up housekeeping. We didn't have much money, but I managed to get another job at Twentieth Century–Fox as a member of a swing gang in the property department for $18 a week. We cleared the sets at night and, working with hammer and nails, dressed them for the next day. The truth of the matter, about which I always have been embarrassed, is that I was a scab. I didn't know it at the time, because the workers who were on strike had no pickets at Fox. I lost my naïveté soon enough, though, when the strike was settled in a few weeks and I was out of a job again. I next got a job in the research department at Metro-Goldwyn-Mayer. I spent most of my eight months there pasting pictures in a book—as costume research for *David Copperfield*—and looking up dates and strange things in the library. Then I was transferred to the film-editing department.

Through my first half-dozen years in Hollywood I was the victim of efficiency experts. All the major studios periodically brought them in from New York. They would arrive, find a payroll of 5,000, and when they left over the weekend the payroll was down to 3,500. I was caught in the middle of that all the time and developed a strong awareness of the need for unions.

In between layoffs I tried writing, and I worked on cheap, Grade B pictures at all the studios. If you were hungry you went to a place like Republic, and the story editor would say, "We have a title—

'Stunt Girl.' Come in Monday with an outline and a few pages of script. If we like it we'll pay you $50 and put you on at $50 a week." You didn't know he was doing that with six other writers; that he would take whichever treatment he liked and incorporate the ideas of the others. I went along with this until even that employment ran out. Then I met Vivian Cosby, who had been a Broadway play-wright and who had turned to writing for radio. She taught me to write for radio, and we collaborated on some movie adaptations for *Lux Radio Theater*. We also did three-minute radio spots—sketches for guest stars—and got $150 for each of those. From there I drifted to the Edward G. Robinson *Big Town* series. I did about six of those at $800 to $1,000 each. The money was good, but I was terribly unhappy. I had been in all the movie departments—casting, cutting, research, story, property—and I had a feel for film making. I wanted to be a director, but I couldn't even get back into the studios.

One morning when I was on my way to Vivian's apartment, where we worked at a large table in front of a window, I stopped first at a drive-in on Highland Avenue and for some reason decided to go inside and sit at the counter. Two fellows were there, going over a racing form, and I eavesdropped and learned there was a bookie place across the street. I went across to it with $26 in my pocket. That evening I met my mother at a cousin's house for dinner. I called her into another room, emptied my pockets, and counted out $3,412. She asked, "What have you been doing?" I said, "I bet on the horses. I couldn't lose." She said, "You're not going back there," and I said, "Oh yes I am. You can keep $3,000, but I'm going back with the rest tomorrow." I did, and came away with another $1,000. The third day I lost what I went back with, but I wound up with $4,200. That really made my life, because I could afford to wait for the kind of job I wanted.

Albert Lewin hired me as his assistant. He had been a producer at M-G-M but pulled away and went into partnership with David Loew for United Artists. They made a picture called *So Ends Our Night* and then *The Moon and Sixpence*. I was general factotum—

story editor, casting director, assistant to the producers, and so on. I was getting very little money, but they gave me a title—associate producer. It seemed I was on my way at age twenty-seven to becoming a producer when, at the beginning of World War II, I got my draft notice.

In lieu of the draft, I applied for an Army commission and was put in charge of a combat photography unit stationed at Camp Crowder, Missouri. From the day I reported there my commanding officer, who had been a captain in the reserves and knew nothing about photography, made it clear to me that he didn't like Jews and, as he put it, "Hollywood Jews in particular." It was a fearful thing to think of going into combat overseas with this fellow, but he told me, "Don't worry about it. Just transfer out. I don't want you around." I tried, but because I had been commissioned directly from civilian life I had to stay there a year. At the end of that time I was transferred to something called "GI Movies" in Astoria, Queens, in New York City. It was a nothing job which called for the creativity of a tse-tse fly. We produced feature films and short subjects for orientation and training purposes. The films weren't particularly interesting, but the by-products were. For instance, it was in the Army that I first encountered narcosynthesis, which I later dealt with in *Home of the Brave.*

I was at an orientation meeting for officers in 1945 when a colonel from Washington told us we could expect to be at war for at least another ten years. The startling thing about that was that, after the meeting, we were standing on the corner of 34th Street and Lexington Avenue when we heard that the atom bomb had been dropped on Hiroshima. The initial reports were that it had killed a million people. We went crazy because we had just heard the war would last another ten years, and now it was going to be over. We got drunk. We cheered from the rafters. The implications escaped me and everyone else except for the scientists who later warned that the chain reaction from a major nuclear explosion could wipe out the entire world.

When I later made *On the Beach,* which reflected my feelings about the bomb, the Defense Department wouldn't lend me the nuclear submarine I asked for. They said I took life too seriously; that if there were a nuclear holocaust it might cause 900 million casualties, but it wouldn't be the end of the world. I told them that was close enough for me, and I wound up having to use a British submarine.

After the war I ran into a Navy man I had met during President Roosevelt's last campaign, for which I had written radio spots. He was one of the Sears Roebuck heirs, Armand Deutsch, and he had the urge to do something creative. He had money, I had technical knowledge, and the combination seemed to be my ticket back to Hollywood as a producer. I prevailed upon him to buy the movie rights to Taylor Caldwell's best-selling novel *This Side of Innocence.* All the movie studios were after it, but we got it, and I formed a company called Story Productions. Deutsch brought in Hal Horne, a publicity and exploitation man and a very good one, as a third partner. Horne publicized it to the sky, but we never made the film. We kept negotiating and negotiating but were unable to make a deal with one of the studios. However, before the film was never made, as it were, we decided—because of some disagreements—that it would be better if we split. They bought out my interest for something like $15,000, and I formed my own independent company. Then fantasy entered my life, just as it had when I went into the bookie place on Highland Avenue.

I had space in my uncle's office in Los Angeles, and William Shenker—whom I knew from before the war—walked in one day. He had seen my uncle's name on the directory in the lobby, came up to see if my uncle could tell him where I was, and I was sitting there. Shenker was a Chinese-food fanatic and wanted to open a Chinese restaurant. His father, a dress manufacturer in New York, had told him, "Look, here's $7,500. Unless you get the restaurant opened in a year, you're going to come to work in the dress business." Shenker had an option on a piece of land and needed another $7,500. He came looking for me to see if I could help him. Instead, I promoted him out of his $7,500, and with that plus what I had I took an option on two Ring Lardner stories, *The Big Town* and *Champion.*

We couldn't use *The Big Town* as a title because of the radio series by the same name. So we changed it to *So This Is New York* and did a movie script for it. I went to David Loew, who had formed a company called Enterprise Productions, which was making films for United Artists, and he agreed to take the picture under his wing with me as producer. He made us cut a couple of hundred thousand dollars out of the budget, and we made the film, which was a satire, for $700,000. George Kaufman once described satire as what closes on Saturday night. This one did—from one end of the world to the other. It was a total failure.

Shenker was a disaster area. I told him, "Willie, they'll probably never let me make another film, but if they do, you've got the same percentage you had in this one." Luckily, I had managed to get *Champion* and *Home of the Brave* financed before *So This Is New York* failed. They both were huge successes, and Willie had a percentage of both. He realized about $300,000 from them and finally opened his Chinese restaurant. The two movies were so successful that I became known as a *wunderkind* producer. I hated the label, because I didn't want to be a producer or a *wunderkind*. I wanted to direct. So there I was—supposedly the wonder-boy producer—making one movie at a time. We made a number of films for United Artists. *The Men*, a film about paraplegic war veterans, was Marlon Brando's first movie. He was wonderful, but it didn't make any money. We made *Cyrano de Bergerac*, for which Jose Ferrer won an Oscar, but we took a terrible financial bath on it. *High Noon* was successful, however, even though John Wayne and others of the gentry accused it of being sort of a communist film.

We made a multiple deal in 1950 to make about twelve films for Columbia Pictures, because it seemed United Artists was about to go out of business. But by then everybody in our company was arguing. They all wanted to do what I was doing—produce—and I wanted to direct. I said, "Okay, I'll play Darryl Zanuck, and everyone else can do their thing. At the end of two years, though—win, lose, or draw—I'm going to do what I want to do and the partnership can end." In those years at Columbia, it wasn't a good financial experience. Also, Harry Cohn wanted me to be the heir apparent, but I didn't want to be. I didn't like him, and he finally ended up not liking me. We made some unsuccessful films for Columbia, but there were some interesting ones too—*Death of a Salesman, Member of the Wedding, My Six Convicts, The Wild One, The Caine Mutiny.* When it was over, Cohn was glad to get rid of me, and I was glad to say good-bye to him.

By then, United Artists had new management. Max Youngstein, one of the partners, ushered me in, and I made *Not As a Stranger.* It was the first film I directed. It made a lot of money, but I don't think it was very good.

If someone today tells me he saw one of my films on television last night, my automatic reaction is, "Yes, but I should have taken that one scene out," or "I never should have let the scene with the father and son run so long," or "I hated the performance of that girl." Yet I get a tremendous, writhing sense of invigoration and glory out of *moments* of my films.

I gravitated in my films toward certain actors who could communicate to the masses what I wanted to communicate. Spencer Tracy was not a social animal with a great sense of social responsibility, but he understood it, and he was the greatest, finest actor I could use to breathe life into ideas in which I believed. He certainly did it in *Judgment at Nuremburg* when he said, "This is what we believe in—truth, justice, and the value of the human being." In *Guess Who's Coming to Dinner* he said, "A lot of people think this black man and this white girl shouldn't get married, but if they are in love they must get married. There are going to be a lot of people who will object, but all I can say is, 'Screw them.'" That was an idea for its time, and it was right on the barrelhead. For those people who thought it was oversimplified, it was meant to be.

In *Inherit the Wind*, Tracy said of William Jennings Bryan, "He looked for God too high up and too far away." I believe that, and I resent the objection to movement and change by formal religions—with the exception of the Catholic Church, where there has been great change. It's quite a while now, but Pope John XXIII, operating in the seat of really black reactionary thinking, opened the door, and the air just rushed in. His contribution was so tremendous that it still cannot be estimated. But where were all the religious groups when they should have been on the picket lines in Detroit or at the gates of Warner Brothers when the dignity of man was on the line? It wasn't a matter of whether that man got $12 more; he was being beaten up for his dignity. All these things seem so simple to me, and I have oversimplified, but I don't know how else to state it in film.

My kind of film maker eludes defining; he's some kind of social animal whose category hasn't yet been presumed or even thought about in terms of where it belongs. I'm not interested in message films—of which I have been accused—because I don't have messages. I do have provocations, thoughts, doubts, challenges, and questions to offer. I question whether the accomplishment in *Rocky* of the little man being able to go the distance is a worthy endeavor. Simply because he goes the distance and gets the hell beaten out of him, does that represent an accomplishment? I don't quibble with *Rocky* as a fantastically good film. The chemistry was there, and emotionally I understand the electric thrill of the little man who says, "I've got to do this. I've got to go the distance," and who then goes ahead and does it. I suggest, though—and this is another story—that it would almost be better if he didn't make the fight at all but became a very good greengrocer. Because in the finale when everybody is cheering, what are they cheering for? It looks to me as though they're cheering for a guy who could be punchy now.

After all these years I couldn't clearly answer any question about what it all means—either my work, my concepts, my ideas. I find myself searching. I don't know what people believe in, and I'm not positive about what I believe in except my own truths which I have inside me. I don't think you can search outside for truth. If you look for truth in as complex a society as we have today you find only half-truths, and from half-truths you can build the biggest lies in the world.

When I was younger I said, "Don't tell me what to do or when to do it or how to do it, and don't tell me what's advisable or inadvisable. I know what I believe, and that's what I'm going to do." A disturbing element in the passage of time is that, if someone makes a statement with which I disagree, I now dissect it—trying to be fair, trying to find a grain of truth in it. That kind of thing may seem to be terribly balanced, but it also impedes the surge forward to override the dissident elements that represent our lack of values.

Patricia McBride

Patricia McBride, internationally acclaimed ballerina of the New York City Ballet, began ballet lessons in 1950 at the age of seven. Her first teacher was Ruth Vernon, in Teaneck, New Jersey, and she completed her studies at the School of American Ballet. While still a student there, she performed for a season with André Eglevsky's Petit Ballet company. In May 1959 she joined the New York City Ballet under George Balanchine and within a few months danced her first solo role. The following year she was named a soloist with the company and in 1961 became a principal dancer at the age of eighteen. She has danced before Presidents Kennedy, Johnson, and Nixon and other heads of state. She performs frequently in guest appearances throughout the country and abroad.

I always had a love of dance. I think it was born in me—my mother was a great jitterbugger—but I didn't know how great a love it was or think about making a career of it until I was twelve. My aunt gave me a pair of ballet slippers when I was three years old. My mother knew that was too young for me to start, but she always had it in the back of her mind for me to take lessons. If you had a little girl, it was one of the things you had her do. I started when I was seven.

We lived in Teaneck, New Jersey, and my mother and my grandmother searched for a good ballet school in the area. They visited various schools and attended recitals before deciding on Ruth Vernon. She had the best recitals and the most advanced students. Miss Vernon had joined the Metropolitan Opera Ballet at the age of fourteen and had been with the company three years before leaving it to go into vaudeville.

I cried a lot when I started lessons, because ballet was so difficult for me. My toes pointed in, although ballet later corrected that. I couldn't understand why I wasn't able to perfect the steps easily. I would get very upset when I couldn't execute a combination of steps. I really was at the bottom of the class. I had so much difficulty that Miss Vernon was sure I never would want to come back, but I stuck with it. It took weeks and weeks of practice, but slowly I improved. The second year, it began to get much easier and seemed more natural to me.

I also had some difficulty with my eyesight, which was myopic, and I became known as "the class squinter." When I was very young I had an ulcer on my eye. My mother took me to many doctors, and they all thought I eventually would lose the sight in that eye, but my mother didn't accept that. Thanks to her determination she found a doctor in New York who healed it. I still remember walking down 125th Street on a Saturday morning after he treated the ulcer with drops. He took very good care of me. Because of the myopia, though, I learned to dance without having a clear image of myself in

Patricia McBride: It was reassuring to have such good friends, especially in those early years—not to be alone but to have really good friends to help you and give you confidence in your going on.

the mirrors at the front of the room. It was more with just a feeling of dance that I learned.

Ballet was most enjoyable for me when we had our recitals in June. I dearly loved wearing the costumes, being on stage, and performing. I just loved it. Miss Vernon would sit on a folding chair a few feet in front of the parents in the audience and smile at all of us up on the stage. She prompted and encouraged us as we danced, and I danced for her—watching her all the time. I loved her dearly. After my mother, she was the person I most admired. By the time I was twelve I was taking ballet lessons every day—thinking completely about dance. It was my whole life. My mother worried a little about that, because she thought maybe I should have been going to parties, but I preferred going to ballet because it made me so very happy. Miss Vernon's lessons were much more important to me than all the parties I could have gone to.

My mother was a very young mother. She was nineteen when I was born and, in a way, grew up with me and my brother Eugene, who was a year younger than I. My father had left us when I was three, and we lived in the same house as my grandparents. My mother worked as an executive secretary in the bank, and I still wonder how she was able to handle all the responsibilities of raising two young children, especially when she was so young herself. She made a lot of sacrifices to give us as much as she did. It really was incredible. She gave me my ballet lessons, and my brother studied the piano. He had taken tap lessons for a year but gave them up. My mother never forced us to do anything like that if we didn't want to, which is very important.

When ballet school closed for the summer I played all the normal kids' games. My brother and I made and sold lemonade. We went bike riding and roller skating. We played tree tag and baseball with the other kids on the block, and for one month each summer my mother took us to the country in Connecticut, where we swam in a lake. I had a great time in the summers, but I missed ballet and couldn't wait to get back, even though I had to work doubly hard in

September after being away from it for so long.

When I was twelve Miss Vernon made me squarely face up to the question of what I wanted to do with my life. I had progressed, she said, to the point where there was nothing more she could teach me. She said that if I wanted to be a professional dancer I must go to New York and get more professional training so as not to waste my mother's money. So the next year I went to the Dance Circle, a school on 54th Street. I took lessons on Saturday mornings and also on weekday evenings. My mother would rush home from work and drive me into the city. Sonya Dobravinskaya was my teacher for eight months until someone told my mother, "You really should send her to Balanchine's school, because she looks like a Balanchine dancer." I didn't want to leave the school, but it was the best thing, because they probably would have kept me there until I was eighteen and then said, "Now you are ready to see Balanchine." That would have been too late.

So I auditioned for the School of American Ballet—the official school of the New York City Ballet company—and received a scholarship. They advised my mother that I also should go to a professional children's school, which would enable me to schedule my academic curriculum around my ballet classes. I did, and from then on I took all my schooling in the city. It was about an hour's ride by bus and subway.

In New York I was surrounded by dancers who were far ahead of me, and that exposure helped me to progress. At Miss Vernon's school my girl friend and I together had become the best students. There always should be others, because it's terrible to be the very best. That was another reason Miss Vernon had said I must go to New York. There always should be others so that you have something to strive for.

In New York I got to see professional ballet performances regularly. I became so intense about dance that if I was free in the evening I went to the ballet. If we didn't get free tickets through the school, we would sneak in. We waited in the lobby and went in with the audience after the first intermission, and we made friends with the ushers, who let us in. At fourteen it was great fun to sneak into the ballet, and I saw some terrific performances—things I still remember and dancers I still remember: Diana Adams, Patricia Wilde, Melissa Hayden. I was seeing and learning so many things during that period, and I cherish those memories.

At fourteen and fifteen I felt that the only way I would progress was to throw myself completely into dance. I had great teachers—Pierre Vladimiroff, Anatole Oboukoff, Muriel Stuart, Mme. Doubrovska, Mme. Tumkovsky, Mme. Dudin. All of them with their different personalities shaped me as a dancer. It was the best training in the world, and I was very, very happy.

The members of the New York City Ballet company trained with the students. There still is no division in class between soloists, corps dancers, and students. We work the same way. So as a student I always had wonderful dancers around as models, and I would then watch them at rehearsals. I was impressed by the other students too, for I never had been in classes where the dancers all were so technically advanced. It made me recognize my failings, but it also made me more determined than ever.

Mr. Balanchine often came to the classes to watch the young dancers who were coming up and who one day would enter the company. I was sixteen when the ballet mistress told me I was to join the company as an apprentice, and I was ecstatic. There were six of us who entered at the same time. We were so happy we all were crying. There were lots of tears and a lot of excitement, and the next season Mr. Balanchine took me as an official member of the company. It had been my dream. There was nothing I could have wanted more.

It was very difficult for me to make the transition that first year. I was the youngest member of the company, and it was the hardest period of my entire career. As a student I had had three hours of ballet lessons a day, and even those three hours were very difficult.

In the company I suddenly was rehearsing for five, maybe six, hours and then performing at night. It was very tiring, and I had my regular schooling besides. It demanded tremendous stamina and endurance. Also, I was nervous because I wasn't sure they would keep me. I was afraid that if I made many mistakes they would ask me to leave. I was very nervous about Mr. Balanchine, wondering, "Will he like me?" My whole life revolved around whether he would say hello to me or whether he would be displeased with what I was doing. But I adjusted and felt more confident, and the nerves went away—although not completely. They never do.

I owe a lot to Nicholas Magallanes. He was my first partner, when I was seventeen. It was a great surprise when Mr. Balanchine chose me from the corps de ballet to dance a section of "Figure on the Carpet," which he choreographed for Nicky and me. Nicky was a great help, and he gave me so much confidence. Time is very valuable to a dancer, but he would say, "Don't worry," and he would take me and rehearse. He was very feeling and caring, and I remember him making suggestions in a most gentle way. He would say, "Why don't you try this?" I had great respect for his taste, and all through my career he continued to give me little hints. He was a wonderful friend, and he gave me so much. Carole Sumner, too, was a good friend who was very helpful. We had been students together, and we joined the company together. It was reassuring to have such good friends, especially in those early years—not to be alone but to have really good friends to help you and give you confidence in your going on.

When I was eighteen I started dancing with Edward Villella. You receive something different from every partner. Eddie was very special, and we had a terrific partnership, and we really grew in dance together. Practically my whole repertoire was with Eddie, and it was a wonderful time for me. I loved dancing with him. He was an extraordinary dancer, one of the most exciting of our time, and he left his mark on so many ballets. Mr Balanchine choreographed many ballets for the two of us during that period.

Toward the end of the 1960s he did a ballet for me for the first time without Eddie. It was "Second Movement Brahms," and it was more lyrical than what I had danced before, and it shaped me in a different way. There was a succession of ballets like that. Then, when I was twenty-five, Jerome Robbins joined the company to choreograph works, and I started to dance differently again because of him. The ballets you dance always change you as a dancer. My husband, Jean-Pierre Bonnefous, whom I met in 1968, joined the company in 1970, and it has been a special experience to dance with him. So many people have a wonderful career or a happy marriage but don't have the opportunity to combine the two. I feel very lucky to have that.

I've been in the company since 1959, and I've never been bored with it. Every time I walk into the room and Mr. Balanchine is there and he starts on a new ballet, it's an incredible feeling. He is a great force in my life. I would be bored if I had to dance the same repertoire day in and day out. It's a rather spiritual experience to be in such a dance company and to be involved with new works practically every season. I adore my repertoire and working with Mr. Balanchine and Jerome Robbins.

You develop great discipline and a strong sense of responsibility as a dancer. Pianist Arthur Rubenstein once said that there's no way of delaying a performance. The curtain goes up at eight o'clock not eight fifteen, and when it goes up you have to be ready. You can't say, "Oh, wait. Audience, wait. I'm not ready." You rarely feel perfect before a performance. There always is something which doesn't feel quite right, but if you let that get to you, you might never go onstage. Sometimes I worry I won't have enough energy to get through, but it seems always to come when I need it.

A dancer's career is so short you don't want to miss a performance. I may have another ten years, and when I reach the end of that there will be nothing left for me as a dancer. So I savor each moment totally. It's not like being an actress who does a film that is there forever. A ballet performance is fleeting. When it's over, it's gone—erased. Some of it remains as a memory, but not the exact details. It's rather sad in a way, but all the beautiful performances I've experienced make it well worthwhile. To be doing something I've always loved to do and to be a success in it is very fulfilling.

Harry Mullikin

Although he began working in a hotel at age fourteen and has continued to do so ever since except for three years in the military service, Harry Mullikin never thought of a career in the field until he was in college. The following year he charted a career path for himself with Western International Hotels. In 1973, at age forty-six, he became president of the company, and in 1977 was named chief executive officer. His company, headquartered in Seattle, Washington, operates fifty hotels in twenty-two countries, including the three largest in the industry. Mullikin also is a director of UAL, Inc., United Airlines, Seattle-First National Bank, and the Sea-First Corporation. The Arkansas-born executive has received the hotel industry's highest honors, and he holds an Alumni Achievement Award from Washington State University.

When I was raised, people stressed that you should become a professional. Professionals were the recognizably successful people, and that was the goal—success. After all, you're supposed to be successful. You're not supposed to be a failure. There can be a big difference, though, between what a person would like to *be* and what a person would like to *do*. At one point in high school I wanted to be a doctor—to be known and respected as a doctor—but I then realized I didn't want to *doctor*. I couldn't stand the sight of blood, and I really had no interest in doctoring at all. It just didn't appeal to me, and I would have been awful at it.

Although I began working in a hotel at age fourteen, it didn't occur to me to stay in the hotel business, because that was not considered a profession. The professions were law, medicine, architecture, engineering, and such. When I finally decided to study hotel management in college, however, my dad was very good about accepting it. He said, "That's fine. Now learn every job in the hotel and learn how to do it better than anyone else ever has done it, whatever the job is, because if you know all the jobs and have done them well it will be a lot easier for you to become a manager."

My father had run a small hotel in McGehee, Arkansas, during the late 1920s and had done quite well. He was only in his twenties, and he also had a small restaurant and a furniture store there. Then some professional gamblers traveling the circuit out of Memphis got him involved in a dice game in one of the hotel rooms, and in one night he lost everything, including our house. It was during the Depression, and there were no jobs. So he took my mother, my brother, and me to Hot Springs, where we stayed with my mother's family while he went to Washington, D.C., to look for work. He got a job with the Department of Agriculture. My grandmother moved north with us, and we started out in a one-bedroom apartment with a fold-down bed in the living room. Each night the bed came down and an old army cot came out. We really had nothing, less than

Harry Mullikin: There can be a big difference, though, between what a person would like to be and what a person would like to do. At one point in high school I wanted to be a doctor—to be known and respected as a doctor—but I then realized I didn't want to doctor.

nothing, but I paid no attention to it, because when you are a kid and all the people in the neighborhood live that way, you think everybody does.

When I was fourteen my dad was transferred to Wenatchee in the state of Washington, about 150 miles east of Seattle, and we lived for a while at the Cascadian Hotel. Since I didn't know anybody in the town, I was around the hotel a lot and got to know the people who worked there. They used to let me run the elevator, and then gave me a job as elevator operator for $2 a day. I worked after school and on weekends and during vacations, and eventually worked as night porter, houseman, busboy, bellhop, room clerk, telephone operator, and bellman. I enjoyed it, but they were all just jobs. I still had thoughts of becoming a professional of some sort and had no idea of making a career out of the hotel business.

When I came out of the service in November 1946 after three years in the Air Corps, I intended to study architecture in college because I always had done rather well at mechanical drawing in school. I got home the Wednesday before Thanksgiving, and I remember my mother said, "Why don't you take it easy for awhile." But that Friday I went down to see my friends at the Cascadian Hotel, and Sunday I started back to work—three days a week as bellman and three days as relief clerk. I also applied right away to Washington State College—Washington State University now. I was one of a ton of veterans trying to get in on the GI Bill. It also was mid-term. So I received an absolute turndown.

A few weeks later I was working the hotel desk on a Sunday morning when a gentleman came down to check out. When I looked at his card, I saw he had signed in as "Claude Simpson, WSC." For all I knew he could have been the head janitor at the college, but I started to kid him. I said, "I don't think I'll let you check out of my hotel because you won't let me check into your college." He asked me what the situation was, and I told him. Then he asked about what I had done in the service and how I had tested out on various things. He finally took my name and said, "I'll see what I can do."

I'm not sure if I ever expected to hear from him again, but I certainly had nothing to lose. Within a couple of days I received a letter from Claude Simpson, director of admissions. It was my notification of acceptance at Washington State.

After the first few months at college, I shifted my interest from architecture to interior design because I had not scored particularly well in mathematics. Then I ran into Claude one day, and he asked what I was taking and how I was getting along. I told him, and he said, "Why don't you stay in the hotel business? You seem to be natural for it." I answered, "I can't do that. I have to have a profession." He simply said, "Why don't you make the hotel business your profession?" So I thought, "Why not?" It seems strange now that it never had occurred to me. I had just been a kid growing up, and since my dad was with the government I wouldn't be going into some family business. I was going to have to make it on my own, and all the influences on me had confined me to considering only the established professions. But after the conversation with Claude I switched my major to hotel administration, although I did keep interior design as a minor.

My father died toward the end of my sophomore year. That left my mother alone, because my brother wasn't at home either by then. She was having a difficult time adjusting, so one weekend I went home and we decided to move to Seattle, where I got a full-time job at the Benjamin Franklin Hotel.

Not completing college never has been a hindrance to me in my career, although things might have been easier had I finished. I think that college does far more for you than teaching you accounting or whatever. Being in college is much different from being in high school. It presents entirely different kinds of social relationships, and learning how to deal with those relationships can be just as important as the academic learning—especially for anyone who winds up in a people-related career.

I always felt that getting along with people was my responsibility. Whenever I wasn't getting along with somebody I felt it was because I wasn't trying hard enough—that I wasn't using the right approach or wasn't handling a certain situation in the proper way. I've always believed that a person should not allow himself to say, "I cannot get along with that human being." When I was a bellman at the Cascadian we had one particularly difficult businessman who always stayed there. He would show up with his trunks loaded with samples, which had to be laid out for the buyers who would come in and place their orders. He was terrible—the most demanding person who ever came into the hotel—and no one wanted to take care of him. For some reason I made up my mind one day that I was going to satisfy him. I wanted to prove to myself that I could. I did, and he was so pleased he gave me a tip when he left. He never had tipped anyone before, but I had done everything exactly the way he wanted it, and I had done it graciously.

The hotel business operates on saying "Yes." For us, "No" is the hardest thing in the world to say. We get what a guest wants when the guest wants it—somehow—and there's no question about it. It's the philosophy of our company, and our decisions are made on the basis of "What does the guest want?" One time the accounting department suggested we give separate checks in our restaurants for beverages and food because it would simplify the accounting procedures. The answer was "No." The guest doesn't want to have to sign two checks. It simply was a question of having the proper perspective, getting right to the essence of things.

The essential question is what can or cannot be done within the framework of a business in which success is based on satisfying the guest. The next most important consideration after the guest is: What does the hotel employee want? How can we design a hotel and lay things out so that employees can do their jobs better and more comfortably, because if the employee is happier, the guest gets better service, and that then lets us make money to take care of the shareholders. If the guests are unsatisfied and the employees are disgruntled in a hotel in which shareholders might have $30 million invested, we're soon going to have an empty building. It also means continually searching for better ways to do things.

I don't believe people can achieve anything without a competitive drive, but I've never been a person to compete with another individual. To me it is more a question of achieving a goal a person sets for himself. I probably have never done anything I am completely satisfied with. I'm not so hard on myself to say I failed at this or I failed at that, but I normally will look at myself and say, "That was pretty good, but if I had done this it would have been better. Next time that 'pretty good' isn't going to be enough."

After my mother and I moved to Seattle and I started working at the Benjamin Franklin, I set out a career path for myself. I wanted to be assistant manager by the time I was twenty-five, executive assistant manager of a large hotel or resident manager of a small hotel by the time I was thirty, manager of a small hotel by thirty-five, manager of a large hotel by forty, and an officer of the company by forty-five. Along the way, I wanted to learn everything I could about the business. I didn't have the presidency as my ultimate goal, because up to that time the president always had been someone with major ownership in the company. That later changed. When it became obvious that the number-one job didn't have to be held by somebody who had major ownership, I changed my sights.

I set those different guideposts for myself for two reasons. First, to have a firm idea of the direction I wanted to go and, second, to allow myself enough time that I wouldn't be restless and champing at the bit. As things turned out, I reached each point a year or so ahead of the time I had allowed. So I was comfortable with my progress and had time to learn every job well. I never concerned myself about how other people were moving. I just felt I was doing as well as I could and concerned myself at each step only with doing my job as well as anyone else ever had. It really does surprise me, though, to find myself president and chief executive officer of a large hotel company. Even though I've been with the company more than thirty-five years and feel I've done every job as well as anyone else, I keep thinking that there should be people out there who are a lot smarter than I am—who should be doing this instead of me.

I always have had an intense curiosity as to how does this work or how does that work and what happens here, which is why I've learned as much as I have about everything I've ever been involved with. I remember my first summer in Wenatchee, when I worked in a plant packing cherries. Part of my job was to keep the filled boxes moving along the conveyor until they reached a point where they passed through a flap and out the other side of the wall. During our morning break on the first day I asked a fellow I worked with, "Where do the cherries go after they pass through that hole in the wall?" He had worked there three years, but he didn't know. So at lunchtime I walked around and found that that was where the lids were put on the boxes, and I saw how they were stacked for shipment. It wasn't that I wanted to see if it was a job I might be interested in, I just was curious. I wanted to know where things came from and what ultimately happened to them.

When I was working at the Cascadian in Wenatchee, we had what we called hand transcripts. Because it was only a 176-room hotel, we posted guests' charges by hand on the backs of their registration cards, but when I got to Seattle they did it by machine. It was a system I didn't know. I worked the day shift, which meant that I started either at 7 A.M. or 3 P.M. On the days I came in at three I got off at eleven, but I had nothing else to do so I would stay until two or three the following morning with the fellow who worked at night and learn how he did the night audit by machine. The next time they needed an assistant manager I knew more about the operation than anyone else. That wasn't the reason I did it, but as a result I got the job.

Another time I had just gotten a job as hotel liquor controller. The fellow who had it before me had moved to a job in the storeroom. When I took it I found it was the easiest job I ever had in my life. He had made an eight-hour job of it, but I found I could do it in four. So I worked with the catering manager for the rest of the time because I didn't know anything about that operation and it interested me.

When they needed a new catering manager, I got the job. I still remember the comment of the previous liquor controller, who told me, "You really lucked out."

There is one basic philosophy which has been extremely helpful to me, and that is to say to myself, "Is there anyone I would rather be?" Not in the sense that someone might answer, "I sure would like to have his car, or his house, or I would like to be twenty instead of forty," but totally—stepping into someone else's shoes and becoming that person with his family, job, friends, outlooks, thoughts, aches, and pains. I think, with few exceptions, a person would have to answer, "No. There really isn't anyone I would want to change places with." What that says, then, is "Am I not fortunate to be a person I wouldn't not want to be? So I guess I am pretty good. Not necessarily great, but pretty good." Starting from there and recognizing what other people have achieved, a person can feel he too probably can do what he really wants to do and—without stepping on anybody, without hurting anybody, without taking advantage of anybody—get what he wants for himself and his family and be happy and contented in doing it.

I remember when I attended my first managers meeting. I wasn't a manager myself but had reached a point in the company where I was invited to attend. It was my first exposure to the fifty other guys all at one time, and I came out of that meeting with two reactions. One was, "What a super bunch of guys. Sharp. Really great." The other was, "I think I can be that good. I think I can make it too." Whether it was self-confidence or whatever, it made all the difference.

Of course there's definitely the circumstance of being in the right place at the right time, and there are situations a person just might not be able to overcome. If an opportunity isn't there, there's nothing a person can do about it, and if a company's not going anywhere, neither is someone who stays with it. It's like a marriage. Someone who has a good marriage ought to stay with it and do everything possible to make it better. If it's a bad one, then get out.

So if a person is getting along all right and moving ahead and fairly happy with a company, I see no reason to think, "Oh boy, I heard about some guy who went with this company and look what he got. I think I'll jump over there." On the other hand, if someone just isn't pleased and knows that what the company plans for him isn't what he plans for himself, he certainly ought to change.

When my oldest son, who is now a professional photographer, was growing up and not knowing what he wanted to be, he said to me once, "I really hope I find something that turns me on as much as the hotel business turns you on." He did—and that's the main thing.

Ralph Nader

Credited as the single person most responsible for the passage by the United States Congress of The National Traffic and Motor Vehicle Safety Act in 1966, Ralph Nader was born in Winsted, Connecticut, on February 27, 1934. Interested in becoming a lawyer ever since his preschool days, he graduated from Princeton University, magna cum laude, *and received his law degree from Harvard. For several years he pursued a private law practice in Hartford, Connecticut, during which time he also wrote and lectured extensively on consumer advocacy issues. Recognizing the need to deal with such issues, and especially vehicle safety, on a national level to achieve enforceable legislation, he decided to carry the fight to Washington, D.C. In 1965, his book* Unsafe at Any Speed *attacked the automotive industry for producing unsafe cars and focused the nation's attention on the issue. Two years later, the United States Junior Chamber of Commerce named him one of the Ten Outstanding Young Men of the Year, and he has come to be regarded as one of the most trusted men in the world. In 1968 he established in Washington the Center for Study of Responsive Law and is the nation's, if not the world's, leading advocate for consumer rights.*

One of the fortunate things about small town living is that the library, the schools, the ball field, the stores, the doctor and lawyer and dentist, and the courthouse and city hall are all within five to ten minutes walking distance. My father owned a restaurant about a hundred yards from the courthouse, and he always talked to the lawyers who came there during the intermissions in their trials. He was very interested in the courts, and justice, and law, and when I was four or five I would walk down to the courtroom and observe the judges and lawyers. I really wanted to be a lawyer from that time on.

My sensitivities about justice were brought about by my parents. They believed a great deal in talking, while we were at the dinner table, and at other times, about public issues. In a nondidactic and a very casual way they communicated to my brother, my sisters, and me that the privilege of living in a democracy involves an obligation to become involved in trying to advance social justice; that there aren't many societies which offer that opportunity; and that it's a failure of obligation if the few people on the planet who can exercise that opportunity, because they live in a democracy, fail to do so. As a result I always assumed that whatever I did had to involve what—in my judgment—would improve society.

Our parents conveyed to us a sense of the preciousness of the freedoms we have in this country. My father once told me, "If you don't exercise your rights, you're going to lose your rights, and if society doesn't exercise its rights, it's going to lose its rights—gradually if not tumultuously."

I had a fortunate choice of parents. I believe the basic personality traits people carry with them in life are in many ways shaped by the family upbringing, probably within the first fifteen years. A person can go on and get a Ph. D., reach a high position, and get a lot of experience, but when that person is in a crunch and has to reflect a level of moral fortitude—which probably is the rarest trait in human society—the response, I believe, is shaped significantly by what

Ralph Nader: My father once told me, "If you don't exercise your rights, you're going to lose your rights, and if society doesn't exercise its rights, it's going to lose its rights—gradually if not tumultuously."

happened in those early years. I think that's the main thing that differentiates people of presumably equal competence and equal experience and talent. X person will be able to stand up against the winds and Y person will not.

I went through elementary school at a time when young boys were beginning to wear long pants, but my mother didn't believe in young boys wearing long pants. So I wore short pants and came under tremendous peer-group pressure. The other boys would say, "Hey, look. He's got short pants." I came home and told my mother, "They're laughing at me." She said, "You go back and tell them you're different and that just because you're different it doesn't mean they should laugh at you." She really was giving me the priceless asset of self-identity—of not being molded like putty by the pressures of any particular mores or fads. I went back and told them what she said, and I remember very vividly it worked like a charm. I then began to point out to them that there never had been a soccer player who wore long pants, that I could run faster than they could, that it was healthier, and that Boy Scouts wore short pants. In effect, I began to think for myself, and that really was more important than the actual subject matter of long pants versus short pants.

One of the most destructive influences on children is the uniform pressure of their peers who believe they all have to say the same thing, wear the same thing, laugh at the same thing, and think the same way. It's tragic because this is a country which permits differences, and these differences should be considered a luxury, an asset to explore. If people had more respect for differences and an understanding that differences bring forth talents of human personality in a fertile way, I don't think we would be such easy prey for discrimination against people because of race, color, and creed. These differences, which have produced so much tragedy in the area of civil rights, are absolutely trivial in contrast with the common humanity and the common potential that bind us.

When I was ten years old, I began going to town meetings, and I noticed there were half a dozen citizens who always stood up and questioned the mayor and selectmen. They had things to propose, and they had done their homework. That impressed me, and I always marveled at how the people who weren't involved citizens treated them as mavericks—as kind of abnormal people—when the reverse should have been the case.

I also read a lot, and I was very interested in Thomas Jefferson and his writings. He had an extremely skeptical view of power and a very up-to-date, as it now turns out, recognition of the need to stay close to the land and of how a society's characteristics develop out of its economic activity—whether it's a production society or one oriented toward service or industry or agriculture. I also admired Jefferson's great principles of constitutional liberty and his versatility. He was a multiple-specialist and able to bridge great areas of human knowledge. Today in particular, which calls for such specialized pigeonholings of the human mind, we can recognize the great value of what he taught us.

On another level, I was very much impressed by the New York Yankee first baseman, Lou Gehrig, because of what he displayed. He was not a naturally talented ballplayer. He had to work at it, especially as a fielder, and by picking up literally thousands of ground balls and throwing them to second and third base he transformed himself into an accomplished star. That impressed me at an early age because most athletes were presented to us as natural talents. Gehrig did it by hard work, and he really exemplified for me what stamina and determination in a chosen pathway will do.

Later in college, I very carefully read the writings of Alfred North Whitehead who was one of the greatest repositories of wisdom. He was a British mathematician and philosopher who taught at Harvard, and, of all the philosophers, I think he perhaps has the greatest pertinence to today's scene.

In elementary school there were two or three very fine teachers who influenced me. They stood head and shoulders above the others, largely because they did not ask us to believe; they asked us to think. Once when I came home from school at age ten, my father asked, "Well, Ralph, what did you do today? Believe or think?" I began right away to think about the distinction he was making.

When you sit in a classroom and merely memorize and regurgitate something the teacher told you, that's believing. If, however, you rebound off subject matter dealing with American history, civics, or whatever and question, and reflect, and come up with your own conclusions after analysis, that's thinking. Too much of our formal education—right through college—is based on students memorizing and repeating what they have been told. One of the main reasons I chose to go to Princeton University was that it had the preceptorial system—with eight students to a professor discussing the lecture which might have been attended by a hundred and twenty students. Although I planned to go on to study law, I majored in languages and Far East politics there. I didn't think it was important what you majored in as long as it was something that gave you a reasoning capability.

One of my most memorable experiences at Princeton involved the spraying of trees with DDT. It showed me how completely oblivious even a university, where many scientists worked, could be to the human effects of pesticides. We, including the people in the sciences, believed that pesticides largely affected pests and didn't affect human beings. When I saw birds dead on the campus green after a spraying of the trees, though, I said to myself, "These certainly aren't pests. They have more complex systems." I went to the college newspaper to try to get them interested, but they too were oblivious. The whole incident taught me several lessons. One is that the most important problems often are right in front of you; they're very obvious if you are willing to see them. Second, I marveled at the limitations of scientists who couldn't relate to a problem not associated with a career role, a grant, or their classrooms. Third, I saw the need for developing a sensitivity to the problem among the victims, the potential victims. Here were college students, some of them in chemistry and biology, who walked between classes while the spraying of the trees occurred. The stuff would spray on them—rather heavily—and they just took it.

When I graduated from Princeton in 1955, I entered law school at Harvard where, during the first few months, I realized that the students were becoming prisoners of the grading system. They were contorting their study of the law to respond to a straight-jacketed version of what was required to advance to the next rung of the ladder. I said, "This is not the way I want to study law." I went down to the poor section of Boston and asked myself, "Where is the law here? Where is the justice here? Where among these crumbling tenements and the poverty is the justice law is supposed to bring? What is the relevance of Harvard Law School to Boston, Massachusetts?" I saw the school as a high-priced tool factory preparing students to practice law mainly in the service of banks and corporations, and I decided to use it as a jai-alai wall. By using that monolithic, rather constrictive structure of legal education to bounce my concepts off of, I developed my own understanding of what law is and should be.

I viewed the primary role of a lawyer as representing unrepresented interests—the interests of the poor, the interests of aggrieved taxpayers, the interests of consumers and of future generations—and I defined a lawyer as a citizen particularly skilled to apply energies for reform.

My mother asked me one time, "What would you be most satisfied with, huge wealth or the feeling that you have helped your neighbors?" We had a little lesson on that for ten or fifteen minutes one lunch hour before I went back to the fifth grade. It was the kind of question we always discussed, and I pondered it walking back to school. When, four or five years out of law school, I met my peers, they'd ask, "What are you doing?" I answered, "I'm trying to get the auto industry to be a little more sensible." They almost always replied, "You went to law school for that?" I'd ask in turn, "What are you doing?" A typical answer was, "I'm working on estate plans for a wealthy Park Avenue couple." I would come back with, "You went to law school for that?" I never have been able to equate a high-paying job in a large New York law firm—serving as someone else's rubber stamp—with the satisfaction of, for example, organizing groups in New Jersey to bring pressure to clean up the rivers and drinking water—which basically involves survival values.

While I was still a student I hitchhiked a lot all over the country. I saw many accidents, and the extent of the injuries sparked my initial interest in auto safety. I was never more amazed than at how people who worked day after day in a vehicle environment never noted the problems with their vehicles until they were pointed out to them. I asked one truck driver about the clothes hook—a few inches behind his head—on which he hung his jacket. The truck was bouncing up and down as we rode along, and I said, "Aren't you ever concerned that you could hit your head on that hook if you got into a slight crash?" He turned around, looked at it, and said, "I never thought about it that way." It was a perfect example of how, without asking simple but critical questions, we tend to look at products the way the producers want us to look at them. We will look at a Chevrolet the way General Motors and Madison Avenue want us to look at it. We'll say, "Look at all that style and ornamentation." We'll marvel at the grill pattern and the hood ornament without asking even the obvious survival question of how much more do those sharp edges subject to serious injury—even at low speeds—the half million pedestrians who are hit each year.

As a lawyer in private practice in Hartford, Connecticut, I was not interested in just making sure that victims of accidents involving defective vehicles got compensation. I was much more concerned with what might be called preventive law—developing safety standards to prevent those injuries from happening in the first place—because, if you don't deal with the structural basis of the problem, you're basically on a treadmill. You can help someone—and that is satisfying—but there's always someone else in line with the very same problem. You have to quest for the source; find what is the source of the problem so you can find the best remedy.

I tried to get some state legislatures, particularly Connecticut and Massachusetts, interested in auto safety, but they weren't big enough to take on General Motors. So after some state hearings at those levels, I realized it had to be done on the national level. Besides, it's a national problem to begin with. So since the mid-sixties I have focused most of my efforts on Washington and federal legislation.

In 1968 we established the Center for Study of Responsive Law. Our society is heavily reliant on law in the sense that it is based on rules with enforceability behind them. That provides for a greater element of potential fairness than exists—in some parts of Asia, for instance—where custom rules. Since I've heavily focused on matters such as corporate power, law is especially important to me—as a means of developing countervailing powers to give people a greater voice as citizens and consumers and to redress some of the excesses of institutional power.

Our work focuses on trying to expand the quantity and quality both of public and private citizen involvement in the major and minor problems of society. Private citizens are people who take care of themselves, raise their families, and earn their livelihoods—all of which is extremely important. The public citizen function, which, of course, can be performed by the private citizen, is one where people look out for their fellow human beings and try to help government be more responsive and efficient, try to help corporations be more humane, and in effect try to improve the society at the local, state, and national levels.

We are trying to develop and promote the instruments of citizen action so that people of all values and orientations can use them, whether they agree with us or not. Our work to get a strong Freedom of Information Act amendment through Congress in 1974 is one example. Now any citizen in this country can ask for certain information hitherto held secret in government, and, if the government doesn't provide that information, citizens can take the government to court. Anybody—liberal, conservative, radical, reactionary, business, consumer, taxpayer—can use this law. It's a perfect instrument of citizen involvement in our society because information is the currency of democracy. The more that people know about what's going on, the more likely they are to be concerned with what's happening and what they should do to make it happen right.

We have put out dozens of proposals relating to citizen action, hoping to involve people in citizen experiences, consumer justice experiences—no matter what their interest—be it property tax reform, more nutritious food, more responsive government, or corporate reform. As we do that, we concentrate on substantive problems like the hazards of nuclear power, the lack of nutrition in certain foods, corruption in government, corporate crime, unsafe cars. In so doing, we demonstrate that instruments of citizen action can make possible the resolution of problems in our society if we work together on them.

There are, of course, difficult moments, such as when we lose a major piece of legislation or a law suit, because so much effort goes into that. But you don't dwell on it. If you go through life figuring everything is going to be nice, you can get rather upset when things are difficult, but if you assume there are going to be problems and difficulties, you rebound much more constructively. My mother once told me that your last mistake is your best teacher. That's a very wise communication because it helps you cope with any possible discouragement, and it gives you an attitude of constantly learning from experience. If, with the benefit of hindsight, we don't think we would have done some things differently, then something is wrong.

Patrick F. Noonan

CONSERVATIONIST

Prior to his appointment at the age of thirty as president of The Nature Conservancy, Patrick F. Noonan worked for four years in land acquisitions for that private, non-profit conservation organization. Born in St. Petersburg, Florida, while his father was in the U.S. Navy but raised in Washington, D.C., he first considered a management position in business before turning to the environmental field because of his interest in land use and the outdoors. In pursuing advanced studies after graduating from Gettysburg College in Pennsylvania, he attended Catholic University and American University in Washington, D.C., where his studies included land use and real estate. He is a member of the American Society of Planning Officials, an associate member of the American Institute of Planners, and a senior member of the American Society of Appraisers. He holds memberships in a number of regional and national conservation organizations.

My grandparents on my father's side were immigrants from Ireland. They came to this country for "a chance," as my grandfather put it, and lived in a flat in New York City. My grandfather worked seven days a week at odd jobs until he finally made his way two hours north to Waterbury, Connecticut, where he became a policeman, and then it was a six-day workweek. He always told me people didn't realize how fortunate they were to have Saturdays and Sundays on which they didn't have to go to work. He never had an education. He just broke away and came to this country to find his own way. My grandfather didn't make much money, but he was proud to be a policeman, and he was a happy family man. My mother's father was an orphan, and he worked his way through law school at Georgetown University. I didn't know him, but I admired him too.

My father was one of five children, and when he decided what he wanted he too went out and did it. He left Connecticut and went to Washington, D.C., where he worked at various jobs to pay his way through law school. In those days if you were smart enough you could go directly to law school without having gone to college. He worked hard and finally got his law degree.

I'm fortunate to have seen my father do what he wanted on his own and to have seen the results of all the time and sweat he put into it. That left an impression—that if you set goals and take the initiative you can realize those goals. It's a lesson I've had the opportunity to apply in areas affecting conservation.

After graduation in 1965 from Gettysburg College in Pennsylvania, where I had a football scholarship and worked at odd jobs for spending money, I wasn't sure what I wanted to do. I always had been interested in business and the free enterprise system because of my father's influence, which is why I took my degree in business management. So I decided to accept a position I had been offered as a management trainee with Sears, Roebuck and Company. I worked

Patrick F. Noonan: I'm an optimist, and I find that I keep going back to the examples of my parents and my grandparents, who found ways to achieve the things they wanted. They set out to make things happen. They didn't just let things happen to them.

in their store in Lancaster, Pennsylvania, spending a number of weeks learning each of the store's various operations. It was interesting, but after nine months I realized that my strongest interest was the outdoors. As a boy growing up in Washington, D.C., I had spent almost every weekend with my parents in the country. My father had bought a hundred acres of farmland in Maryland during the 1940s, and we used to go there to fish and hunt and hike. When I got older I camped there on weekends. I have fond memories of those times. They left a tremendous imprint on my life.

While I was still in college my father sold the land to the local county for a park, and at that time I met the fellow who handled the purchase for the county. His name was Jack Hewitt. Jack was the only person I knew in the conservation field, and one day toward the end of my nine months with Sears I drove down to Washington and went to see him. I told him, "I really don't enjoy what I'm doing. I think I would like to get into work involving the land and the outdoors, but I don't know how to go about it." Jack said, "It just so happens we have something. It's a job as an assistant for acquisitions, working in the parks department, but it doesn't pay much. Do you want to take a shot at it?" I told him I didn't care what it paid; that I just was interested in getting into the field and finding out as much as I could about it.

The parks department was part of a bi-county agency charged with planning the expansion and growth of Montgomery and Prince Georges counties, which abut Washington. I worked on acquisitions for parklands but also got involved in land-planning activities, including zoning, variances, and such. It involved all the classic clashes—land-use problems—which arise where urban development encroaches on rural areas. After three years I felt it would serve me well to learn what I could about the theories behind land-use planning, and I enrolled at Catholic University for graduate work. I went five nights a week while working days with the parks department. I was fortunate that my wife Nancy shared my desire to continue my education, and she worked to help meet the expenses.

Land-use planning was a brand-new graduate program at Catholic University. I felt strongly that planning was the key to proper land-use decisions. In planning terms, conservation always has been what's left over. Even in the graduate program we did not have a single course in ecology, and I don't think any school did at that time. We were taught to accommodate for growth—lay out the development, provide housing, roads, schools, and all the related commercial and industrial areas—and what was left over we colored green. It's only in recent years we have learned the importance of first identifying our critical natural lands so as to provide habitat for wildlife and other species. I remember a time when there were two trout streams in Montgomery County, Maryland. One of them was on my father's property, but after he sold the land and I got back from college I learned it had become polluted. It was the stream in which I had fished as a boy, and I couldn't understand how people could allow that sort of thing to happen.

When I graduated from CU in 1967 it was as one of the first five graduates from the program with a master's degree in land-use planning. By then I also had my own real estate office. I had been just a year into my graduate studies when I decided to leave the parks department, because I had become frustrated with the politics involved in government planning activities. I also wanted to find out how the real world ticked on the other side of the fence in terms of real estate dynamics. Why do investors buy land? How do zoning decisions get made? Who are the investor groups? Why do banks lend money and insurance companies participate in joint investment ventures? In school we were getting only theory, and it seemed that the best and quickest way to learn the dynamics would be to do so firsthand. In Washington you could just walk in the front door and take the examination for a real estate broker's license, without having to go through any intermediate steps. After failing the test the first time and spending many hours studying, I went back two months later and passed.

With my broker's license I opened a small office in downtown Washington and started selling real estate and working with developers on their plans, mostly for residential developments. After almost two years of that, which was shortly after I received my degree in planning, I went back to night school—this time at American University for a master's degree in business, with a major in real estate. I took all the courses I could in real estate appraisal because I wanted to become a qualified appraiser to understand still another aspect of real estate dynamics. My business and studies all fit together nicely for about two years—it was hard work, though exciting— but I wasn't getting personal fulfillment out of the real estate business. Real estate brokerage generally is strictly dollar-oriented. I see nothing wrong with that, but I wanted something more for myself because I believe we have been put on earth to be of service to others. Because of this basic belief, coupled with a love for the outdoors and the realization that true success comes only when one is doing what one enjoys, I felt my education and practical experience could be put to better use in protecting America's natural heritage.

At about that time, when I was thinking of going back into conservation work, an article appeared in the Washington *Post* about The Nature Conservancy. It sounded like a unique nonprofit membership organization involved in land conservation, and seemed to combine everything which I was interested in and skilled at. Here my values, my education, and my professional experience could be brought together. I wrote to the Conservancy headquarters in Washington and was able to arrange a meeting. They had no openings at the time, but a short while later they offered me a position as a trainee in land acquisitions and operations. The salary wasn't much. In fact, I had to take a cut in income, just as I had when I went from Sears to the parks department, but it was a field in which I strongly believed.

The Conservancy is involved specifically with the protection of unique habitats and natural preserves, but, when you shake all that out, much of its operations involve land-use dynamics, real estate dynamics. Saving a piece of land requires complex negotiations and an understanding of federal and state tax laws, zoning, real estate terms, finance, and related fields before the land can be brought under protective stewardship as a refuge or a park. It's not a simple subject. In fact, even with my background it probably was a full year before I was an effective person at the Conservancy. During that year, though, I really began to understand what was happening to our natural world, and I benefited enormously from the association with so many wonderful people from all walks of life who shared a strong commitment to the success of the Conservancy's efforts.

In 1973 the president of the Conservancy left, and the board asked if I would be interested in taking the job. At the time I was only thirty. There were three individuals to whom I turned for advice and counsel in arriving at a decision as to whether I should accept the challenge the job posed. They were the two past chairmen—Alex Adams and Warren Lemmon—and Wallace Dayton, the current chairman at the time. Although they were from widely different geographical areas of the country and had different professional backgrounds, each had played a major role in laying the foundation for the Conservancy. With their support and encouragement I decided to accept the post.

All the chairmen under whom I have served—including John Andrus, who now holds the position, and William Blair, Jr., who preceded him—share a fundamental dedication to the Conservancy's work. Each also brought business acumen to the running of a nonprofit organization. Their sound judgment and thorough understanding of the organization necessary to direct a corporation have been major assets. Some management approaches we have adopted were rarely if at all practiced before in the nonprofit field.

Each environmental organization is unique. Each has a different message, a different focus, a different kind of staff, board, and membership. The Conservancy basically is the real estate arm of the conservation movement, and because of that it also is the arm most involved in creating and maintaining nature preserves and wildlife sanctuaries through direct acquisition. We have a truly interdisciplinary staff—Ph.D. ecologists, wildlife management people, forestry school graduates, and lawyers. We also have a large group of MBAs, which is rather unusual in the conservation field, but their business backgrounds are indispensable. The real success of the Conservancy, in fact, can be traced directly to the dedicated men and women who, while from different backgrounds, work as a team toward mutually agreed upon land conservation objectives. Where we really are unique, as a result of that, is in attempting to balance the emotional aspect of conservation with the economic realities of what is possible—knowing what can and cannot be done.

The greatest problem we all face insofar as the environment is concerned is the awesome one of supply and demand. People have tremendous demands now, with more leisure time, more disposable income, more forms of travel accessible to them for recreation and other pursuits. And we have more people coming. The population growth projections are there, and they are very real. Those people will have to live somewhere, and that means homes, vehicles, and everything else that goes with our current standard of living—including the waste which accompanies it. Yet we have a limited base—a fixed land area and, in many cases, fixed water sources, such as aquifers. We have to find out how to have clean air and clean water and provide the experiences that people seek when they go to a national park or other preserve. That's very difficult. On just one two-day weekend at Yosemite in the fall of 1976 when I was there, 60,000 people visited the area. That creates water problems, security problems, transportation problems, and sewage problems. For the solutions, we must look to planning. The environment must be protected. We all live in it, we all breathe it. We fish in it, we drink it. So we have to protect those systems which provide clean air and water.

If life is a learning experience, which I think it is, then individuals and society as a whole must build upon that experience and learn from it. What is going through the mind of the developer who has a $1 million land investment and $10,000-a-month payments on that money? He has to sell his land. He has his backers screaming at him. Meanwhile the land planner is telling him, "I'm sorry, Johnny, but we're going to have to tie you up for another five or six months until we work this thing out." That's just conflict. I'd rather be involved in the avoidance of conflict and for that you have to understand another person's value system. A recurring problem for the conservation community is the opposition it arouses because it hasn't properly explained its value system and frequently fails to take into consideration the conflicting demands of people on the lands involved.

Many conservationists don't know what's important to protect and save. They base judgments on emotion, not on hard facts. To me, haphazard conservation can be worse than haphazard development, and many people feel that the conservation community has failed to establish its priorities. If we are to have a livable environment in the future, we have to set priorities. We have to identify at the local, state, and federal levels which streams, which marshes, which wetlands, which fragile zones must be protected, explain why they are important, and then publicize it. In doing so we can have land conservation come first rather than last and, at the same time, channel private development away from important life-supporting areas.

The key to a successful corporation is its planning. It knows where it is going. It knows where its markets are and is able to react quickly to new opportunities. The same thing should exist in terms of conservation. We have to accommodate the necessary day-to-day demands of the population on our natural resources while at the same time striving to preserve conservation values, and we have to do it in such a way as to avoid conflict. It can be done if we plan.

I'm an optimist, and I find that I keep going back to the examples of my parents and my grandparents, who found ways to achieve the things they wanted. They set out to make things happen. They didn't just let things happen to them.

Rosser Reeves

ADVERTISING EXECUTIVE

Rosser Reeves, former chairman of the board of Ted Bates & Company, spent some thirty-five years in advertising. Born in Danville, Virginia, but raised primarily in Richmond, he entered the New York advertising world in 1934—with $7 in his pocket. In 1940, he, Ted Bates, and others founded their own agency, which became the fifth largest in the world, with annual billings in excess of $500 million. During his career, Reeves, who was the most highly paid copywriter and executive in his field, wrote Reality in Advertising. *It propounded the principles for which* The New Yorker *dubbed him "The Prince of Hard Sell." That book, although written for businessmen, went on the best-seller lists and has been reprinted in eighteen languages. Rosser Reeves retired from Ted Bates & Company in 1965—on his fifty-fifth birthday— as a multimillionaire. He since has opened his own agency, Rosser Reeves, Inc.*

Law was my first conscious career interest. I was unaware as a young man that what I really wanted was writing, even though I had been editor of two high school papers and of the University of Virginia literary magazine and had worked one summer as a newspaper reporter.

I think the only reason I wanted to go into law was that I had read and learned so much as a child that I found classes at the University of Virginia rather boring. I was studying things I already knew. In fact, if you were on the dean's list—which, as I recall, meant maintaining an average of 95 in all your subjects—you didn't have to go to class. So I never went to class, and I stayed on the dean's list.

Law intrigued me because I knew nothing about it. They had a system at the University of Virginia under which you could apply the first two undergraduate years toward your bachelor's degree and enroll in law school for the last two. But if I had gone into law I would have been a terrible misfit unless I had become a criminal lawyer. Sitting in an office writing corporate briefs would be foreign to my nature; but criminal law seemed to offer a life of action. So as a sophomore I enrolled for law school. Actually it was a childish concept from reading books like *The Great Mouthpiece* and following newspaper accounts of Clarence Darrow at the Scopes trial in Tennessee. It was as vague as that.

To get credit for my sophomore chemistry course, I had to write a paper. The Francis P. Garvan Foundation had an annual awards program for chemistry students from all the major colleges in the country. This involved writing a paper on one of six themes: "Chemistry and Its Relation to Warfare," "Chemistry and Its Relation to Agriculture," and so on. I chose the easiest, "Chemistry and Its Relation to the Enrichment of Life," a subject you can approach from any viewpoint.

All the other students at the university were doing formidable papers so stuffed with research and formulae that they were *chemis-*

Rosser Reeves: *Along the way I got fired from two or three agencies because I wouldn't write advertising their way. I was very hardheaded, and I kept shifting agencies to try to find those that knew what they were doing.*

try papers. I put mine off until the last night. I had a book in my library called *Creative Chemistry*, by Edwin E. Slosson, a very famous book in 1929. I just cribbed from it and wrote a paper in layman's English. It took about twenty-five minutes, but it won the national first prize, $500, which was an enormous sum of money then. This got a great deal of attention and front-page articles in the Richmond *News Leader* and the Richmond *Times-Dispatch*. At the time, there was a remarkable young banker in Richmond, Thomas C. Boushall. He read about it and wrote to ask for a copy.

Boushall had come South from New York to start the Morris Plan Bank of Virginia. All the other banks at the time were commercial banks. They made loans to big businesses and corporations. Boushall didn't deal with companies, but extended personal loans to individuals. It was a new concept, and he had a communications problem. He thought, "If this kid can make chemistry sound simple, he ought to be able to make banking sound simple." So he offered me a job editing a house organ that the bank's tiny advertising department published. It coincided with the end of the school year. I didn't know what else to do, so I took it as a summer job. I thought it would be amusing.

Within months the stock market crashed. My father was a poor Methodist minister, and it just cleaned him out. He had invested what money he had in stocks, and he had no money to send me back to college. The whole world was coming unglued. So I went to Mr. Boushall and asked, "Will you make me advertising manager?" He said yes. It was as incidental as that. I fell backwards into advertising.

In 1933 I got hold of a copy of a new book by John Caples of Batten, Barton, Durstine & Osborne entitled *Tested Advertising Methods*. It convinced me that I did not know what I was doing and that, if I wanted to learn, I had better get myself to New York. Mr. Boushall, who by that time was a surrogate father, said, "I'll give you our account. Take it to New York and get yourself a job." I had two suits, $7, no job, but the bank's advertising account. They were spending $60,000 a year, and I traded it to an agency called Cecil, Warick & Cecil for a job at $34.50 a week.

When I arrived in New York I had one goal—money. In twenty years I was a multimillionaire running one of the largest advertising agencies in the world. Very few professions, if you can call advertising a profession, give a young man a chance to make really huge sums, and that opportunity still exists in advertising. By 1939 I was knocking down $35,000 a year, which was a giant salary for a young man in those days. When I was twenty-nine years old I was living in one of the greatest mansions in Westchester. I sold it ten years later to buy one of the most beautiful waterfront houses within five hundred miles of Manhattan.

Bruce Barton, one of the founders of Batten, Barton, Durstine & Osborne, which some wit said sounds like a trunk tumbling downstairs, also was a preacher's son. Henry Luce of *Time, Life,* and *Fortune* was a preacher's son. One day Luce and Barton were having lunch and discussing the canard that preachers' sons all go to hell, become alcoholics, bums, or sexual perverts—and so they decided to find out what does happen to preachers' sons. Wherever it was they did their research—*Who's Who,* the *American Directory of Directors,* or what—they found that there were more sons of preachers than of any other single profession listed in their reference books. Barton later did an article on this for the *Saturday Evening Post* and offered some theories on why it was so. One was that all preachers' sons grow up in homes with libraries filled with books and they all get magnificent educations. He also concluded that they achieve so much because they once were poor and a dollar is important. That's why I wanted the money, and why I got it.

My father was a Methodist fundamentalist, a real Bible pounder, to put it mildly. But he was a classicist. He was a professor of Latin and Greek. He was a college president before he felt the call to go into the ministry. So it was a highly literate household in which I grew up. But you wouldn't find Voltaire in my father's library. You wouldn't find H. L. Mencken or Robert Green Ingersoll. And the people who had the most powerful influence on me to blow me out of this Methodist fundamentalism that my father believed in—a literal heaven, a literal hell, a literal Jonah being swallowed by a literal whale, that whole routine—were Voltaire and Paine and Mencken. The iconoclasts. I read them all when I was ten, eleven, and twelve years old, at the public library.

My father had a library of about 8,000 to 10,000 books. Aristotle, Plato, Socrates, Aristophanes, Cato, Cicero, Juvenal, Pliny, Claudius—shelves and shelves of classics. I was ten before I discovered that there were any books except these. When I broke free of that, it was like a drowning man coming up for air. But it was a terribly literate family and a beautiful base. My two sisters and I grew up reading and writing, and one of my sisters became one of the most famous of the radio soap-opera writers. She did *Stella Dallas, Helen Trent,* and so on, and she made a great deal of money out of it. I had published some poems and short stories in national magazines—just sketchily, because I was a very young man—but I wanted to write, and I did. But I still was unaware that I was more interested in reading and writing than I ever would have been in law—or medicine, chemistry, or anything else.

I did have an early introduction to advertising. When I was fourteen the Richmond *Times-Dispatch* ran a contest offering cash prizes for the best advertisements written for certain products. I wrote six, sent them in under assumed names, and won the first six prizes. They weren't very good. I think I won because they were neatly typed. But still there never was a deliberate attempt on my part to enter advertising. It was a natural way for me to flow, but it was a turn of events that channeled me that way.

One day in the Hunt Room at "21" the heads of the twelve largest advertising agencies met for lunch to discuss an industry matter. It was over rather quickly, and the conversation turned to "How did you get started in advertising?" Not a single one of us at the table had ever intended to go into the business, which recalls the story of the fly that lit on the nose of the dog of Robert, the Duke of Normandy.

History records that Robert was lying in his palace courtroom when a fly lit on the nose of one of his dogs. The dog growled and slapped at the fly with his paw. This recalled to the duke's mind the pleasures of the chase. So he ordered out his retinue and went hunting in the forests of Normandy, where he encountered a gigantic stag. Having the fastest horse, the duke became separated from his retinue. He did not get the stag, and on his way back to the castle he passed the daughter of the tanner of Falaise bathing naked in a brook. He put her on the crupper of his horse, took her back to the castle, and made her his mistress. She bore him an illegitimate son who became William the Conqueror. Now, if the fly hadn't lit on the nose of the dog, the dog wouldn't have slapped at it and growled, the Duke of Normandy wouldn't have gone hunting, he wouldn't have encountered the stag, he wouldn't have seen the daughter of the tanner of Falaise, there would have been no William the Conqueror, no Battle of Hastings in 1066, and no Anglo-Norman dynasty. There would have been no British Empire or First or Second World Wars, and the world would have been entirely different. I think that the turning points in most people's lives are accidents. I got a beetle in my pants once on the way to the country club in Richmond. I got out in front of the headlights to take off my trousers and get the beetle out. It was during Prohibition, and a friend who was with me said, "This is George Street's house. I know him well, and he has some marvelous liquor." Well, we went in, and I met George Street's daughter. We were married in 1934 and had four children and are still married.

Chance is a major ingredient in the conduct of people's lives, but it certainly shouldn't all be left to that. The minute I arrived in New York, I immersed myself in advertising. I discovered that everybody did it a different way and that there was no science to the advertising business at all. I began to read the advertising theoreticians. Claude Hopkins was one of them, and his books had a powerful influence on me. They made me realize that what Cecil, Warick & Cecil were doing was amateurish; that they really didn't know their business. I left and went to an agency that did, a hard-sell outfit called Ruthruff & Ryan, a famous agency in its day. Then after about three and a half years I went with the other hardest-sell agency in the business—Blackert, Sample & Hummert—as copy chief, which was a hell of a job for a twenty-seven-year-old. Along the way I got fired from two or three agencies because I wouldn't write advertising their way. I was very hardheaded, and I kept shifting agencies to try to find those that knew what they were doing.

It was easy for me to get jobs, because there weren't many good copywriters around and I had rapidly established a reputation as a good writer. But since there were so many people working on the accounts I was put on, I didn't feel that any of them really were mine. I was almost like a bricklayer on a construction crew, and didn't become an individual operator until I met Ted Bates and, with some others, we started our own show.

Throughout all this time, I was still in search of the principles of advertising success. In law or medicine or engineering, you learn your profession by learning everything that everybody before you had known. This has never been so in advertising. In every decade there's a new crop of advertising people who keep inventing the wheel—which is rather stupid, because the wheel was invented many years ago. The result is that, if you go to ten different advertising agencies with the same problem, you get ten different answers, because they all have different philosophies. One wants to do it cute and charming. Another wants to do it another way—and so on, right down the line. But there's only one way to do it—Claude Hopkins helped me see that—and that is by using the same hard-sell philosophy used by the drug companies and the package-goods companies. After all, what works once should work again. For instance, there are not a hundred different ways to take a brain tumor out of your head. There's one way better than all the others, and if you have to have a tumor removed you are better off with a surgeon who follows a proven procedure rather than having three doctors working over you, with one going through the ear, one through the eye, and the other coming up through the throat.

When I put forth my philosophy and principles of advertising success in my book, *Reality in Advertising*, it split the advertising community right down the middle. Half of them loved it, and they usually were the younger writers. The other half hated it, because, if the book was right, what they were doing was wrong. So they had to hate it.

Ted Bates and I based our approach on the philosophy of hard sell, and to say that it worked is putting it mildly. We started with only a handful of employees and grew to be the fifth largest agency in the world, with annual billings now in excess of $500 million. For twenty-five years we did not lose a client, and even clients who didn't like us, because we were running a very unpopular form of advertising, were afraid to leave us. We also were the pioneers who explored the new medium of television. We just took it over. That's why we became so big, so rich, so fast. It was a lovely new medium—motion and sound as well as copy—the greatest selling medium of all time. We became the world's number-one expert in it.

Bill LaPorte of American Home Products, who later became chairman, came to me one day with a problem: Anacin sales had leveled off at $17 million a year and stayed there for five years. I wrote him a television commercial, and it took his sales to $54 million in six months. It was a 59-second "motion picture" that cost $8,200 to produce, and it made more money than *Gone With the Wind*. You can't argue with that. For Forrest Mars, I wrote a commercial in one morning—"Which hand has the M&M chocolate candy in it?"—and he had to build two new factories.

The only proof for any advertising campaign is actual sales in the marketplace. A panel of creative people from twenty-five top agencies once picked what they considered to be the three worst commercials of all time. As it turned out, two of their choices had been the most successful in terms of generating sales.

It's interesting that in my lifetime no one ever has asked me whether I had a college degree or not. As far as advertising schools are concerned, I don't believe there is one that teaches you anything at all about advertising. It has been my experience that they are run either by pedagogues who know nothing about advertising or by bad copywriters who like to do something in their spare time. As a matter of fact, the minute I heard someone had gone to advertising school I refused to hire him, because I knew they had put so many bad ideas in his head. The same thing applied with people who just had been floating around the advertising business. I was better off taking young graduates from liberal arts colleges and teaching them myself rather than getting high-priced copywriters from other agencies who had too much to unlearn. Give me any college kid or high school kid with a facility with words and an analytical mind— and a person has to be analytical to be a good nonfiction writer— and within two years I can make him into a good copywriter by providing the precepts to follow. The only other thing that is required is willingness to work hard with total commitment, because any profession—if you're going to be good at it—will swallow up your life. Advertising swallowed up my life completely. It almost killed me.

In a practical way, Ted Bates had a powerful influence on my life, more than any other single man. He was about ten years older than I was, a great deal smarter than I was, and a great deal calmer and more controlled than I was. There really have been two surrogate fathers in my life. One was Thomas Boushall, the banker, and the other was Ted Bates. Bates and I had a relationship where one plus one equaled eight. He liked to run the company and deal with the accountants, the lawyers, the clients. The business aspects always bored me. I liked to run the creative department and never gave it up, even when I was chief executive officer and chairman of the board. In fact, Bates and I, late in our life together, had quite a row over it. He was getting old and didn't want to keep running the agency, and I refused to do it, because I wanted to run the creative end. I did, right up until the end when I retired on my fifty-fifth birthday.

Pete Rose

Born in Cincinnati, Ohio, in 1941, Pete Rose signed his first professional baseball contract the day after he graduated from high school. He played three seasons in the Cincinnati farm system before joining the Cincinnati Reds in 1963. By the end of the 1977 season he had become the greatest switch-hitter in baseball history with 2,966 hits, surpassing Frank Frisch's total of 2,880. That total also placed him fourteenth on the all-time hit list, and his 204 hits in 1977 also tied Ty Cobb's record of nine 200-hit seasons. His 162 games that year extended his consecutive game streak to 652—the most among active players in the major leagues and tieing Frank McCormick's record for most consecutive games ever played by a Cincinnati Red. With nine home runs, he also set a National League record in 1977 for most home runs—144—by a switch-hitter.

I often wonder how people outside Cincinnati might receive me years from now if I wind up playing in an Old Timers game after I make the Baseball Hall of Fame. I think about whether they will boo me as they do now or give me a hand. I lead the pack in boos whether it's Los Angeles, Chicago, or New York. I ask people why they boo, and the answer I get is that they don't like aggressive people. I've always believed that if you're going to go out for something you should go all out, but in today's society people tend to get upset about people who are super-enthusiastic, super-aggressive. But I've proved that people who are aggressive can achieve without natural ability.

I saw the first scouting report done on me after my first two months in the minor leagues at Geneva, New York. It said I couldn't hit left-handed, I couldn't run, I couldn't throw, and I couldn't make a double play. I can't throw well, but I get the ball there. I can't run well, but I'm one of the best base runners in the game; I always take the extra base. Although I can't run as fast as some guys, I'm the only player in the history of the National League to have led it in doubles for three straight years. At one point in the minor leagues I hit 49 triples in two years—30 triples in one year and 19 the next. And during the 1977 season, having batted left-handed more than right, I broke Frankie Frisch's record for more hits than any switch-hitter in the history of baseball. The guy who wrote that scouting report got fired. He had to.

The way people are today, it seems nobody wants to work on his weaknesses. It never ceases to amaze me that during spring training or before a game, the guys who can hit are always in the batting cage. The guys who can field are out taking ground balls. I know I can hit, so when they switched me to third base in May 1975 I spent all my time taking ground balls. Day in and day out, at age thirty-three, I took twenty-five to thirty minutes of ground balls before every game. A twenty-three-year-old kid could have gone out there

Pete Rose: *If you're going to give two and a half hours to a baseball game, you ought to try to win. Someone's got to win, and someone's got to lose. So let the other guy lose. It's as simple as that.*

and taken ground balls for an hour; I had to work so damned hard it tired me out—although I wouldn't admit it—and I made the All Star team at third base that year and ever since.

I could have told them to go to hell when they sent me to third after several years as an All Star outfielder, or I could have been a complete flop and been sent back to the outfield by the end of the day, but it was a question of pride. I think the difference between the guy playing to win—the guy playing hard every day—and the guy with an "I don't give a damn" attitude is pride. I've got more than the average man's share of it. Anybody can go out there and go through the motions, but even though we might be losing 8–0 in the ninth inning, if I can break up a double play or take an extra base I'll do it. I do it instinctively, because I've done it so many times for so many years.

You keep hearing the old cliché "It's not whether you win or lose, it's how you play the game." That's 150 percent against my philosophy, because in professional sports winning is everything as far as I'm concerned—so long as you play clean and don't try to hurt anybody. I try to instill in my son, as my father did in me, that winning is what makes it fun, and, with as many games as we play during the baseball season, if you don't have fun it's just a drag-out bore. My son plays Knothole ball in Cincinnati, the same as I did as a kid. They don't have Little League there. The kids get more out of it today, though, because they emphasize winning more, which they should. If you can teach kids how to win, it will help them in life later on. If you're going to do your homework, you ought to try to get a good grade. And if you're going to give two and a half hours to a baseball game, you ought to try to win. Someone's got to win, and someone's got to lose. So let the other guy lose. It's as simple as that.

You also want to teach kids to say "Nice game" to the opposition when they lose. I won't say anything bad about the other guys, but I've never been able to compliment them. I could the next day, but not right after it happened. When I lose a game I like to sit and contemplate what happened and figure out why I lost, so that the next time the situation comes up I won't lose again if I can help it. If I lose a World Series, I won't be in the winner's clubhouse congratulating the team after the last game. I'll probably call up each player individually the next day, though, and say, "Nice going. I enjoyed playing with you."

I've played organized baseball since I was nine years old. I was very fortunate to have had a father who played amateur sports. I think I got from him all my enthusiasm and desire to win, but he never made me do this or that. He just exposed me to the games, and I grew up digging sports. I was ball boy on his basketball team. I was bat boy on his baseball team. I was water boy on his football team. He worked in a bank, but he played a lot of football, including pro football with the old Cincinnati Bengals team, which operated for just one year in the 1930s. He was the only non-college player on that team, because he had to get a job after high school, but a lot of people said he would have been the best college football player ever to come out of Cincinnati. He worked hard, and he played hard. He wasn't a very good baseball player, because he didn't have good eyes, but what he lacked in ability he made up for in determination.

Another influence on me was my mother's brother, Buddy Bloebaum, who played baseball in the Cincinnati chain and who later, as a scout, signed me to my contract. He didn't have his biggest success in professional baseball until he became a switch-hitter when he was thirty. So when I started Knothole at age nine, he and my father got their heads together and decided to make me a switch-hitter right from the start. My father worked it out with my first coach. He told the coach that if I was made to switch-hit he never would take me away from the team for a family vacation in the summer. He made the coach promise I would bat left-handed against right-handed pitchers and right-handed against left-handed pitchers no matter what the circumstances—even if the game was on the line or if it was a championship game. The coach agreed, so I became a switch-hitter at a younger age than probably anyone else ever had.

I practiced a lot on my own. The Knothole coaches did a great job, but you can't become a great player practicing twice a week. Besides, when I was a kid all we had to do in the summertime was play stickball or baseball. Today's kids have a lot more available to them, such as cars, and the key to the younger athletes who are making the teams is that they really are dedicated, because they had so much more to give up in order to practice. I wasn't a poor kid, but I used to watch *The Millionaire* on television each week and hope Michael Anthony would knock on my door. He knocked on someone's door every week and gave away $1 million. Whoever got it could keep it as long as he didn't tell anyone about it. I used to think I would put tape across my mouth if he ever gave it to me. My whole childhood was great, though. I got a new baseball glove every year and a new basketball. I lived right on the Ohio River and used to work on the ferry boats, and I could go down there to fish or go boating. There were woods behind my house, and we would go up in the hills to ride horses and camp out. I wouldn't trade my childhood with anyone, because I had everything I wanted.

In high school I was much better at football than baseball. I played it a lot, because my father did. I'm like him in every way, although in one respect it almost hurt me. We both developed late physically for our ages. I was captain of the high school freshman football team and played left halfback even though I weighed only about 130 pounds, but because I was so light I didn't make the varsity when I reached my sophomore year. You had to be invited to go out for the varsity, and they asked the guy who played behind me at halfback. It didn't make much sense, and I was heartbroken and so discouraged I skipped school a lot that year. I flunked because I missed so many classes, and I had to repeat my sophomore year. By then, though, I had grown enough to make the team. I played halfback, and the guy who had been jumped over me, and who then was a junior, played the other halfback position. In my junior year I made the All City team, but as a senior I was ineligible for sports. We were allowed only six semesters of eligibility for varsity ball, and I had used them all up by repeating my sophomore year, even though I didn't get to play the first time through.

My uncle had become a scout for the Reds by the time I graduated in 1960, and if it hadn't been for him I probably never would have gotten a shot at professional ball. There was no chance of my playing college football, because in those days they weren't looking for college halfbacks weighing 155 pounds. That was light for baseball too, but my uncle convinced the Reds that everyone in my family matured late physically, including him and my father. So he really is the one who got me the opportunity to play baseball. He signed me to a contract the day after I graduated. The Reds wanted me to wait until the following year, since it was so late in the season, but I wanted to join right away, and they took me. I signed on a Saturday morning and left for the Geneva Reds the following Monday.

It was my first time out of Cincinnnati. I played only two months because it was so late in the season, and that's when the scouting report was done on me, but it didn't bother me, because I knew I was in the process of maturing physically. I came back from Geneva weighing 165 pounds. My second year, when I went to the Tampa Tarpons, was when I hit 30 triples, and I came back from there weighing 175 pounds. After my third year in the Cincinnati chain—at Macon, Georgia—I weighed 185, and the following year I was 195 when I went to spring training with the Reds on a Class A contract.

When I broke in with Cincinnati in 1963 everyone resented me, although I didn't realize it until a couple of years later when Earl Lawson, a sportswriter for the Cincinnati *Post*, mentioned it. The Reds had won the National League pennant in 1961 with Donald Blasingame at second base. The following year he hit .282, which is pretty good for a second baseman. It had been his best year ever. So when the Reds went to spring training in 1963 the whole team thought they had a chance of making it to the World Series with him at second. That was the position I was trying out for.

The team stayed at the Causeway Inn during spring training then, away from downtown Tampa, and one night about eighteen or nineteen players were in the lounge when Earl Lawson gave each of them a sheet of paper. He told them, "I want all you guys to write 'Yes' or 'No' if you think Rose is going to make the team." They all voted "No," except for Donald Blasingame. When we started the season and I was there and Blasingame wasn't, they all were mad at me. It was a very cliquish team that year. They all hung together, and they shut me out. I didn't take much notice of it, because I was on a cloud just being in the big leagues. I did think that the fact I didn't have a coat or a great wardrobe might have had something to do with it, but I didn't give a damn about that. The only ones who did associate with me were the black players, Frank Robinson and Vada Pinson. In fact, the front office called me in one day and said, "You're associating with the black players too much."

One night in Chicago I came in at a quarter after twelve and my roommate had locked me out. I just went upstairs and slept in Vada's room. Frank wasn't on that trip because he was in Cincinnati having his arm worked on. The next morning Vada asked if I wanted to eat with him, and I said sure. He always had room service because he hated to go down to the coffee shop, just as I do now. So he bought it for both of us, and I remember it cost him $12. I thought back to that a couple of years later when Earl Lawson told me what had been going on, but I remembered the incident because it was the first time in my life I ever had room service. Because of all that, I was determined that what had happened to me would never happen to any other player while I was with the team. I go out of my way to treat the young players well. I don't want any of them to feel neglected, because that can hurt the team.

The last game of that rookie year was one of the biggest highlights ever for me because I played against Stan Musial, one of the greats of the game, on his last day as a player. We were at Busch Stadium in St. Louis, and I was standing closest to him during the festivities before the game. He gave me an autographed ball that day which read "Continued success for many more great years." That day is right up there with the other highlights, such as my first All Star game, winning the batting titles, playing in the World Series, winning the World Series, and receiving in 1976 the Hickock award, which goes to "The Professional Athlete of the Year" from among all the sports. These all were especially rewarding because I know how hard I had to work to get there.

When I sat in the clubhouse that first year with the team, I never thought I would become as good a player as I am—that I would be as aggressive as I am or that I would ever have had a shot at Frankie Frisch's record. I've played more games than anybody in Cincinnati. I've batted more times than anybody in Cincinnati. I've scored more runs, more total bases, more hits, more doubles, and every time I play a game in a Cincinnati uniform it could be another record. But I'm not conscious of that all the time, because you don't play for yourself in baseball. What you do as an individual helps you get paid, but the important thing is what you do as a team. I don't want a ball hit to me to go right through my legs and have the pitcher lose a game, because that guy is making a living pitching, and I'd rather strike out five times than make a stupid error. I dropped a pop-up when we were playing the Dodgers in Los Angeles in a nationally televised game in May 1977. It was the first time in fifteen years I dropped one. I flipped my glasses down, and when I did I lost it. It hit in front of me. I couldn't find a hole big enough to crawl into. But I've never made an error when I wasn't trying 110 percent.

Everything I've got and everything I ever will have is because of baseball. I don't know what I would be doing if it hadn't been for baseball, but I do know I would be enthusiastic and aggressive at it. In 1975 I opened my first restaurant in Cincinnati, and I was there every night. I spent endless hours there. I was concerned about how people would feel when they left, because they weren't going to tell their friends they were at the cook's restaurant or at the waitress's restaurant. They were at Pete Rose's. That's where the pride comes in again.

Alvin Toffler

AUTHOR

Born in Brooklyn, New York, and a graduate of New York University, Alvin Toffler has spent most of his working life as a professional writer. Because he wanted to write a novel when he graduated from college, he and his wife spent almost five years working in factories in the Midwest to "touch the people." He then worked as a journalist for sixteen years before the publication of Future Shock, *of which more than six million copies are in print, with translations in about twenty languages. He is a worldwide lecturer, and has a new book in progress. After his first writing job with a trade magazine for the welding industry, he became an editor for a daily trade union newspaper. He then went to Washington, D.C., as a reporter for a Pennsylvania newspaper and did extensive free-lance work for magazines. In 1959 he returned to New York as an associate editor at* Fortune *magazine for two years. He is the author or editor of six books.*

I always have been interested in the future, all the way back to when I was a child reading Buck Rogers in the comic strips. In one of my earliest memories I still can see myself coloring Buck Rogers pictures.

From the time I was seven I knew I wanted to write, mainly because I then thought writers got free tickets to ball games, but I never took a course in journalism. Moreover, when I was a student at New York University, I made a distinction between journalism and the literary life. College promoted a kind of pathological elitism. We were taught that there was a hierarchy; that certain forms of writing are better or more important than others, regardless of quality. There was a distinct pecking order—in much the same way that classical music is considered better than rock. Literature and fiction were better than nonfiction; nonfiction, better than journalism. So I looked down my nose at journalism. That was for poor struggling hacks, whereas we "aesthetes" and "radicals" had more serious work to do.

My uncle and aunt were much closer to me in age than were my parents. They were bohemians, the family intellectuals, and they were very influential in shaping my early development. When I began writing poetry they both encouraged me, and my interests began to lean more strongly that way. They said, "Don't be ashamed of writing poetry. It's a good thing to do. Write poetry. Keep writing." My parents were supportive too, but worried. They regarded my idea of becoming a writer as potentially disastrous. If I had realized my father's ultimate dream I would have become Chief Justice of the United States Supreme Court. In my Dad's view, that was the single most important job in the world. But his realism told him I should aim for something more achievable: teaching. My mother felt the same way. Teaching meant steady work and security. During the Depression years when everybody else was hungry, teachers worked, and it was clean work.

Alvin Toffler: After I had been with Labor's Daily *for two years, I felt I had learned just about everything I could and that it was time to move on again. That has been consistently true in my career: leave when you've learned.*

My father worked at a sewing machine in the fur industry until I was a teen-ager. Then he began to buy and sell furs, and we eventually moved onto the standard upward-mobility track—from the working-class section of Brownsville to the bottom reaches of the lower middle class in Flatbush. In the course of changing high schools during that move, I wangled my way onto the staff of the school paper as a cartoonist. I was told I couldn't be an editor or a reporter because I hadn't taken journalism courses, but once on the staff I became the paper's managing editor within a few months. By the time I entered New York University I wanted to become a literary critic or a political columnist, but I hadn't the faintest idea of how to go about it.

The most valuable thing college did for me was to throw me up against a lot of people who were actively thinking and to plunge me into New York City's Greenwich Village at that particular moment in history. It was an exciting place. The veterans were coming back from World War II. There were 65,000 students at NYU, a lot of them mature ex-GIs. We spent more time having bull sessions in Washington Square, which was the NYU campus, and in local restaurants, bars, and people's living rooms than we did in the classroom, and I learned far more from that. Fortunately, the school was so loose, disorganized, and crowded that no one missed us.

In retrospect I'm not sorry I went to college. I don't feel the time was wasted, but it could have been crunched into two years instead of four, and they could have done it in a very different way and much better way.

We aspiring writers—and there were many of us—hungered for contact with professional writers. It was criminal that the university never provided that contact. There we were growing up in New York City, the publishing capital of the world, a city crawling with writers—advertising copywriters, dramatists, public relations men, radio scriptwriters, novelists, poets, critics—and one would think that somewhere in the course of four years the college would have put young people interested in a literary career into face-to-face contact with honest-to-goodness writers. I would have settled for the least-known professional in town. The closest I ever got was attending a lecture given by a novelist visiting the campus and taking a course with a guy whose claim to fame was that he once had written a story for *Ladies Home Journal.*

During my freshman year I started a literary magazine called *Compass Review.* I met my wife Heidi in Washington Square Park and with her help and the help of other people we organized a network of kids on something like forty campuses. The college provided an office and typewriters, and we got young people from all over the country to send us poems, articles, and stories. The magazine became increasingly political and radical and absorbed an enormous amount of our energy. It came out irregularly—whenever we sold enough ads—but many people who wrote for it went on to become professional writers.

In 1950, the year after we graduated, Heidi and I left New York and moved to the Midwest. We were suffused with idealism in those years. The United Nations had been formed, and there seemed a chance for the whole world finally to become just, kind, and marvelous. But there still were people who were poor in the U.S. Young and romantic, I wanted to make contact with "the people." Like everyone else I knew, I wanted to write the Great American Novel, or its nonfiction equivalent. I didn't see how anyone could write meaningfully about life, however, or communicate with anyone but Ph.D.'s unless one got out and touched the people, sharing the way they lived and worked.

Steinbeck had picked fruit; we decided to go into the factories to find the proletariat.

We chose Ohio because that's where the steel was being poured, where the foundries were, where the autos were built. I worked night shifts, day shifts, and swing shifts. I became a welder and a millwright. I fixed machines in foundries, drove trucks, built Chevy station wagons. I learned how to use my hands and talk with Americans who got up at five in the morning and carried lunch buckets to work. Heidi became a shop steward in an aluminum foundry. All this horrified our parents, who had worked so hard to spare us a life of manual labor, but it was an extremely valuable, formative experience for us. It shook me out of the sheltered lower-middle-class milieu in which I had been raised and gave me a better idea of what actually went on in the world.

I got a realistic picture of how things *really* are made—the energy, love, and rage that are poured into ordinary things we take for granted. One day I carried a sixty-five-year-old woman out of a punch press in which she had just lost four fingers. She screamed, "Jesus and Mary, I'll never work again." In her agony, with four bleeding stumps, that was all she could think about. You never forget that.

All during those years I wrote abortive short stories, political tracts, and poetry—none of it published. Occasionally I would submit something and collect the expected rejection slip, but I continued to write, hoping I someday would connect. Later I knocked on the doors of newspapers and advertising agencies, looking for any kind of work that involved the printed word. I got laughed at, but you need to be able to accept rebuff without cracking. I kept looking through the yellow pages and going from door to door. Finally I came across a job with a trade publication—a welding magazine. The editor didn't give a damn about my college degree. He just said, "My God, you know how to weld?" He asked me to write a sample article describing a process I knew. I did the piece, and he hired me. It was my first writing job, and I got it not because I knew how to write, but because I knew how to weld. Even today I can't pass a welder at work without feeling a twinge of nostalgia for the brilliant blue beauty he sees through his mask.

I took a cut in pay and worked there for several months and then began thinking of moving on. I started reading *Editor & Publisher* and applying for jobs on the daily newspapers listed in the classified section. My attitude toward journalism had changed as college and its values faded into memory. I saw an ad for a reporter to cover the labor beat on a Midwest daily. Having worked in factories and knowing something about unions and management, I applied. I didn't even get an answer. Then I saw an ad for a job as feature editor of *Labor's Daily*, a newspaper published by the printer's union, the ITU. I applied and miraculously got the job. We moved to West Virginia, where the paper's headquarters were.

Then as now, Heidi was very much a part of what I wrote. She shared in all my decisions about what job to go for and what to write, what not to write. For example, she urged me for years not to write a book until I had a book really worth writing. At first she would merely listen as I read my manuscripts to her and would grunt if she didn't like something. As time went on she became a superb editor, extremely articulate, able to suggest new transitions, tighter structure, clearer exposition. She still critiques all my ideas, arguing with me and forcing me to sharpen or reject them. She has been my intellectual partner from the word go, willing to gamble on the free-lance life and not only understanding what I am trying to do but compelling me to understand myself in the process.

As to how people get a start in this profession, Heidi often tells the story of a young fellow and his wife we met in Belgium. He was correspondent for *The New York Times* in the Low Countries, and we asked him how he had gotten the job. He told us, "My wife and I dropped out of journalism school in Missouri. We asked ourselves where news was going to be made. The European Common Market had just been set up, so we figured Brussels. We simply packed up, went there, and began sending stories to all sorts of publications, none of which had a staff in Brussels." In a matter of months this young fellow, still in his twenties and without a journalism degree, was *The New York Times* correspondent there. He went where the opportunity was. So did we when we made the decision to pack off to West Virginia.

Labor's Daily was the only national daily the labor movement ever published. The idea was to create a truly labor-oriented daily to offset the *Wall Street Journal*. As feature editor I advertised for free-lance material from professional journalists all over the U.S.

because I had to fill two pages a day. I got a lot of material, but the quality of much of it was so poor it encouraged me and helped establish confidence in my own ability. I knew my material was better.

After a year the entire staff of the paper moved to Iowa because the union had a printing plant there. It was Christmas of 1955, and twenty of us, after putting an issue to bed on a snowy Friday night, left in a caravan of cars. We arrived in Iowa on Saturday night or Sunday morning and put out the next issue that Monday. It probably was the only time in history a daily moved halfway across the country without missing a stroke.

The editor was a marvelous Louisianan named "Scoop" White. He was just a few years older than the rest of us, but he did a lot to make his stable of editors into competent journalists even though we were young, inexperienced, independent, and irreverent. We continually poked fun at George Meany, and we carried a lot of page-one stories about Martin Luther King, editorializing against racism. Some Southern locals of the union threatened to stop paying dues if we didn't cut it out, but we got away with it anyway, in part because we worked for so little. In fact, had the union carried out its repeated threats to fire us, it would have improved our standard of living significantly.

I learned a lot from that experience. It exposed me to a whole set of problems—automation, health and welfare issues, economic questions, political issues. I wrote and wrote and wrote every day and edited the copy of others. I soon began to realize something was happening in the country which the national press had not yet detected. Changes were occurring in society which were not being reported adequately.

After I had been with *Labor's Daily* for two years, I felt I had learned just about everything I could and that it was time to move on again. That has been consistently true in my career: leave when you've learned. Moreover, at that time I felt the action was going to be in Washington.

While working for the paper in Iowa I had sold some free-lance pieces to a Pennsylvania paper, the York *Gazette and Daily*, and in 1957 they had an opening for a half-time reporter in Washington. As soon as I heard that, I hurried to fill the spot. Again it was for coolie wages, but I snapped it up. I went with the best wishes of my friends in Iowa, for by then the labor paper was having financial troubles and was forced to cut back its Washington bureau. So I arranged to do stories for them from there on a free-lance basis.

When we arrived in Washington I began filing for the *Gazette*—and for everybody else in sight to make up for what I had lost in wages by taking the job. I went to the National Press Club building, which consists of what seems like hundreds of offices—many of them little one-room cubicles—in which the Washington bureaus of newspapers and magazines from all over the country are located.

I took the elevator from the top floor and worked my way down along all the corridors, stopping in at every office and saying, "I'm a writer. Can you use me?" I also discussed story ideas I brought with me. I went through the entire place from top to bottom and got just two bites: a free-lance assignment from the *Christian Science Monitor* and a research assignment for a writer who was working for the New York *Post*. But I also got to know a lot of people.

Soon I was doing articles for the Washington *Star*, *The Nation*, the *New Republic*, and many other papers and magazines in addition to the *Gazette*. Although the pay from the *Gazette* was poor, the job was very valuable. Not only did it take me to Washington and thrust me into the political mainstream, it also gave me invaluable experience as a writer. Apart from filing news stories on White House press conferences, my chief job was to do a column and write two or three interpretive articles a week. These pieces very often took the form of short magazine articles. Unlike news stories, they had not only a beginning, a middle, and an end but a distinct, fairly complex internal structure. Although I didn't realize it at the time, these were training me, sharpening my craft, preparing me to be a real magazine writer.

Heidi and I sat down one night and figured out that I had filed about 15,000 words that week for approximately $95. It was getting to be an impossible treadmill, and I decided to try longer, more thoroughly researched pieces that paid more. Heidi and I bought up stacks of magazines off a newsstand, read them carefully, tried to think about their needs, the audiences they spoke to, and the subjects they seemed interested in. Then we brainstormed up a list of possible story ideas for them.

I took a few days off and went to New York to call on the editors of the big national magazines. Fortunately, some of them were old-time newspaper people who leaned over to give me a break. They listened to my ideas and rejected most of them but agreed to try me out on one or two on a speculative basis. One editor who was especially helpful was Ben Merson of *Coronet*, who had been an editor at the New York *Journal-American*.

Because of Merson, *Coronet* became a very important base for me, as it was for a lot of writers. It paid $300 to $400 an article—as did *Pageant*, then edited by Ray Robinson—which seemed a lot to me, but the work was hard-driving.

The magazines were hungry for copy, and I completed a piece every week or ten days. I'd get up in the mornings and go to Capitol Hill, cover some hearings, and interview a bunch of people, taking copious, almost verbatim notes. In the afternoon I'd dash across town to the Department of Commerce, the Department of Health, Education and Welfare, the Federal Trade Commission, or the White House. Then I staggered home and wrote until late at night. My bedtime reading consisted of congressional committee reports. I would do a colorful personality profile of some politician—Johnson, Kennedy, Goldwater, Humphrey—for *Coronet* or another popular magazine and then do a long piece of political analysis, based on information from the same interviews, for one of the intellectual magazines.

All that legwork, the constant interviewing and research, provided the equivalent of a graduate school education—more, in fact, and better, because it wasn't specialized. One day I would cover hearings on disarmament. The next day it might be agriculture, and another day some labor problem. I wrote stories about chemical additives in food, stories about water pollution, stories about the military-industrial complex—about many things which later became major issues but which in those days were not.

By covering all these different topics I became keenly aware that the government was increasingly out of touch with what really was happening in the country. All sorts of trends were under way that were going unobserved—changes in the culture, in family structure and organizational structure, changes in technology. We seemed to have no detection mechanisms for scanning the horizon for change.

The government seemed to be spending 99 percent of its time on housekeeping for yesterday, voting to keep last year's programs going. It was more concerned with what had happened than with what was happening. So I wrote an article, a think piece called "The Subterranean Revolution," suggesting we were entering a revolutionary period of subsurface change in America. I submitted it to a few magazine editors, but none accepted it—and they shouldn't have, because the piece wasn't developed. I had not yet thought out the idea adequately. So I set it aside; let it marinate.

After three years in Washington it was time to push on again. I had mastered the short-article form. I knew my way around Capitol Hill. I felt ready to tackle something new. By then I no longer was writing for the *Gazette* but free-lancing mainly for the popular magazines. I had gone from researching and writing every day or two to doing articles that required a week, ten days, or two weeks to prepare. I liked that, because it gave me a chance to think deeper and dig deeper. But they still were short articles, and the necessity of paying the rent meant I had to write fast. Gradually I shifted over to magazines that paid more and let me spend three weeks to a month on an article. But even these still limited me to 2,500 to 3,000 words, and some subjects were just too complicated to deal with in that short a space. I felt I needed more space for more complex ideas. So I wrote to *Fortune* magazine in early 1959. *Fortune* ran much longer pieces—articles of 6,000 and 7,000 words—and its writers could spend months to research and do them properly. Moreover, *Fortune* was a serious magazine. Even though I disagreed with some of its editorial policies and still do, its articles were carefully documented and definitive, and in those days it did a great deal of imaginative social reporting. It covered the major urban problems of that era. It dealt with science and technology and even the arts.

So I submitted a list of free-lance ideas. *Fortune* was intrigued enough to write back and invite me to stop by when I was in New York. But Hedley Donovan, who was then its managing editor, also made it clear that *Fortune* seldom bought free-lance material. Would I be interested in joining the staff instead? That November I moved back to New York after ten years away and joined *Fortune* as an associate editor. In effect, however, I continued to function as a free-lancer. I would spend a week in the office discussing an assignment and going through the morgue to see what background articles were available. Then I'd disappear for a month or two and return with the finished piece, having traveled and worked at home in the meantime.

I learned a tremendous amount in the two years I was there. I learned what it means to write with all the resources at your command—unlimited access to long-distance telephoning, travel expenses to almost anywhere, research assistance, statistical backup, anything you needed to get the story. I also learned what careful checking requires. At *Fortune* the fact-checking was obsessively good, and I learned how to check, recheck, double-check, and triple-check a fact, a quote, a statistic. In that sense it changed me professionally, and I became a much more careful writer as a result of having been there.

I left *Fortune* in 1961 because, again, I felt I had learned what there was to learn. I could handle highly complex material. I could structure very long articles. I concluded, however, that one had to be on the staff twenty years before he could have any influence whatsoever on editorial policy. I also observed what happened to people who worried too much about security; how they cut off their own opportunities.

I saw people who stayed at *Fortune* only because of the profit-sharing or the retirement plan. They felt trapped and grew to hate their jobs, and in turn grew to hate themselves for what they were doing. I wanted none of that. I left and went back to free-lance writing, where you take your chances and live from article to article. You live on your wits, talent, and energy, with no security at the end of the line. I liked the sense of gambling and the freedom that went with it. Moreover—and this is critical—so did Heidi. She preferred this life to the regular, predictable paycheck.

With the *Fortune* experience behind me and being a better writer because of it, I began working for magazines like *Good Housekeeping, Playboy, True, Ladies Home Journal, Reader's Digest*. Almost always the pieces I wrote dealt with social issues. I did others, too, on less important topics because I had to stay alive, but I learned even from them. I never wrote an article that didn't enrich me or teach me something I hadn't known before.

A very important event occurred during that period when in late 1962 I was invited to participate in a month-long seminar in Austria—the Salzburg Seminar in American Studies. I was one of four Americans who lectured before about fifty Europeans who were professionally involved in the media. That experience internationalized me, and I realized from that point on I never again could write for an exclusively American audience. It made me recognize that some of the trends altering the United States were at work elsewhere as well and that problems which seemed to be uniquely American were not. Later, when I wrote *Future Shock*, I consciously did so with the outside world in mind and made sure that the book included research from European and other countries. Had it not been for the Salzburg experience, *Future Shock* would have been a much more American book, and it probably would not have wound up being translated into twenty or twenty-five languages.

During the course of my free-lancing in the 1960s, I had tried for a long time to sell some editor on my doing a profile of Kenneth Boulding, an economist who was then with the University of Michigan. I had followed his work and admired him for years. Boulding interested me because I've always looked for those thinkers who are not in the mainstream, who operate outside the system, who poke at the system and come up with novel insights. He was one of them, and he had a sweeping view of world change. I went from one magazine to another, but the editors all turned me down on the grounds that Boulding was too little known; that his name on the cover of a magazine wouldn't sell copies.

I got absolutely nowhere until late 1964. Robert Cowley was then the editor of a magazine-to-be. It was called *Sky* and was to be distributed on airplanes—the forerunner of today's in-flight magazines. Cowley asked me to do a piece for his first issue. I told him I had a lot of assignments and was very busy but that I'd be willing if he would let me do a profile on Boulding. A piece on a leading economist made sense to Cowley because *Sky*'s audience would be composed mainly of traveling businessmen. So Cowley gave me the go-ahead. I flew out to the University of Michigan and spent a couple of days interviewing Boulding. I then came back to New York to write the piece. I literally just had written the first paragraph when the telephone rang. "Stop writing," the voice said. "The *Sky* has fallen in." The magazine would never be published.

That was the end of my profile on Boulding, but *Horizon* magazine, which was published by the same company, asked me to do an article about the future instead. The editor wanted my own feelings about change and what was happening in the world as a result of it. In the course of writing that article, which I titled "The Future as a Way of Life," the concept of future shock crystallized. I remember exactly how it occurred.

I was doing research on the dislocations caused in people by shifts in culture—what the anthropologists call "culture shock"—and one of the psychologists I interviewed was Dr. Rachel Gittleman-Klein. During a telephone conversation with her an analogy occurred to me: if a person could be dislocated geographically in space, a person also could, in effect, be dislocated in time; if one could have "culture shock," one also could have "future shock." That analogy changed my life.

The *Horizon* article allowed me finally to get down on paper some of the ideas I had been struggling with since my ill-fated essay on the "subterranean revolution." There was an electric response to the article. It was 1966, and there was a sense of change in the air. The Berkeley campus had blown up. A President had been assassinated. People were reeling with change. *Horizon* received more mail than it had ever received in response to a single article. It was apparent that there was a subject here which needed far more investigation and more space than an article could provide. It needed a book.

I went to work on the book almost immediately, but in my mind the title was the same as I had used in *Horizon*. I resisted calling the book-in-progress *Future Shock* because I was not prepared to organize the entire book around that concept. But as the manuscript grew over a period of five years—while I kept writing free-lance articles on the side to pay the bills—it focused more and more on that central concept, and it became more and more apparent that that was what the book was going to be about. That *had* to be the title.

Future Shock had far more impact than I, Heidi, my publisher, or anyone else ever dreamed it would. It exploded in country after country. People buried me under an avalanche of mail. Presidents and prime ministers quoted it. People wrote music about it, named lipsticks and racehorses Future Shock. Reviewers analyzed it in every language. Universities taught courses about it. And still do.

But there are some things *Future Shock* didn't do. There are things I didn't understand when I wrote it, things I naturally see differently now, for I've grown and changed and the world has changed radically in the interim. So looking back at it now, while I think it holds up well, I also see its weaknesses. I think its main theme is as valid as ever, although I would write some parts differently today. Still, I resist rewriting it and probably will to the grave, because I believe a person has limited creative energies and I would rather create anew than rework yesterday's product.

Like much else I've written, it was at its time the hardest thing I'd ever done, but it looks easy in comparison to the book on which I am now working and which I find an even greater challenge. I think most writers will agree that writing gets harder instead of easier. We tend to bite off ever bigger mouthfuls. As a result, writing becomes more complex and challenging.

It sounds presumptuous, but I want to change the world, and, despite the difficulties in that, it's why I write. I'll settle for small changes, but my purpose in writing is to influence behavior, to influence society and its development, and to explain what I've learned. And as my understanding deepens, the problems of explanation become even more difficult. So I work to learn and learn to work. For me that means working is better than not working. I would much rather go to Indonesia or Australia as a working writer than as a tourist, and I feel that way about life. I'd rather go through life as a writer than as a tourist.

Bari Wood

NOVELIST

Raised in Evanston, Illinois, Bari Wood graduated from Northwestern University in 1957 with a degree in theatrical studies. Initially she pursued a career in the theater, but then became an editor of medical journals. With no background in fiction writing she began to write her first novel at age thirty-five. The Killing Gift became a best seller and was produced as a made-for-television movie. Noted author Merle Miller hailed her second novel, Twins—co-authored with Jack Geasland and released in 1977—as "Extraordinarily exciting! Both suspenseful and filled with psychological insights." New American Library purchased the paperback rights for a near-record price of $1 million, and Bari Wood now is working on two other novels.

I can't say at what point I decided to write a book. I think I had the idea for a long time, but I didn't start until I was about thirty-five.

You have to be clear on what your motives are and what you want to do in writing a novel: whether you want to make a living at it, whether you want to make a lot of money, or whether you really don't want to write at all but want to go to a psychiatrist or find a lover and the writing is a substitute. I wanted to make some money.

First I got a tape recorder and tried to dictate my thoughts into it, but that made me too self-conscious; it was just me and the microphone. I didn't want to invest in a typewriter, so I began writing longhand. I set myself a goal of three pages a day, and I wrote at night after work. Every night. It took me more than two years, but I finished it. Once I start something, I won't stop until I've finished it. Sometimes it was twenty minutes, and I was able to watch television. Sometimes it was three hours. But I wouldn't stop until I finished three pages.

When I decided to write *The Killing Gift*, I tried to figure out what would be salable. I was very clear about that, very honest. There was no trick to it. It was just a matter of looking at the best-seller list and reading some of the books on it. They were spooky and creepy and filled with murder, sex, and violence. So you write a book that's spooky and creepy—with murder, sex, and violence. An intricate plot isn't essential. Most modern novels simply are interesting stories, and choosing an interesting story is just a matter of good judgment.

A person doesn't have to be a born writer to make a living at it. There are plenty of novelists around today whose work is not great, but it is entertaining and enjoyable, and they are making a living. Of course, there is literature—the really great writing that involves the communication of deep, complicated feelings. That requires an inborn talent, but the writing to tell a story—the writing to draw characters, the writing to describe events—often requires nothing

Bari Wood: *I set myself a goal of three pages a day, and I wrote at night after work. Every night. It took me more than two years, but I finished it. Once I start something, I won't stop until I've finished it.*

except the will to do it. There's nothing mysterious about it if you are clear about what you think, clear about what you want to say, and have the discipline to get it down on paper.

People who really want to write generally can if they forget the formalistic thing and concentrate on their thoughts. It's just like writing business letters. I used to have a terrible time with them because I was caught up in the idea of what it was to write a business letter—which was all the "wherefores" and "heretofores." But once I got past that, it no longer was a problem. It was simply a matter of concentrating on what I wanted to say.

A lot of people do not write to communicate. When I was involved with technical writing, I found that many people write to obscure. For whatever reasons, they want to keep their thoughts to themselves. Maybe they want to impress others with how much only they know, and so they write in a way others cannot understand. Maybe they think that, if their writing is simple and direct, people will think their thoughts are simpleminded. Others are not really clear themselves about what they think, and they want to hide that. Some of the best writing actually is the simplest in the world. It's so clear, so direct, it's fascinating. I truly think more people can write than do.

I remember when I was just about eight years old I started to write a book, and I read a great portion of it over the telephone to my mother. She was out for the evening, and I called her wherever she was and read it to her. I was interested in reading too, and my favorite book was *Jane Eyre*. As a young girl I was most interested in becoming an artist. My uncle Louis Ritman was quite a well-known painter, a Post-Impressionist. I wasn't bad at it, but I wasn't exceptional. I guess I knew all the time that I couldn't excel at it; there always were people around who were better. So then I started wanting to be an actress.

When I was growing up, there was nothing I'd rather do than go to the movies. I loved them all, and I was in a lot of children's plays before high school. When I was in high school I won an acting contest. It was a publicity gimmick by a repertory theater. I had read about it in the newspaper. The prize was a part in one of their plays, *Watch on the Rhine*. I still wanted to act when I entered college, and I enrolled in the theater school at Northwestern University. I lost interest in it, though, because I came to feel that acting was a horrendous way to make a living. So I began to take courses in playwriting and theatrical management.

While at Northwestern I wrote what I think was the best piece I've ever done—a term paper on the humanism in *King Lear*. It was very well thought out. I knew exactly what I wanted to say, and the writing simply was communicating. A lot of the kids in the course cribbed their stuff from Granville-Barker and Bradley. The professor was a well-known and respected Shakespearean scholar, and he failed them all. When he got to my paper he called me in and said, "I cannot find where you copied this from. Please tell me." I was so delighted, so complimented, that I blushed and laughed. When he saw I was flattered, he realized I had written it myself and gave me an A-plus.

After I graduated in 1957 I bummed around for a year—traveling mostly through the South. It was the beatnik era and the thing to do in those days. By the end of the year I had reached New York. My car was shot, but I had had it in mind to wind up there anyhow. I had a lot of friends in New York and vague thoughts of getting into theatrical production. At first I took some odd jobs, such as demonstrating products in Macy's department store. Then I got a job at the Fourth Street Theater. The stage manager was a friend of mine, and they needed someone to re-cover the seats. Then the owner gave me the job of treasurer.

I quit after a few months and took a job for the summer at the Meadowbrook dinner theater in Cedar Grove, New Jersey—again as treasurer. I was a bit of a gambler and got involved in an on-and-off game of hearts with the actors. After a few weeks I got pretty good, saw how much money I could win playing cards, and really got involved. Within three months I had won $5,000, and a friend and I opened our own theater in Cliffside Park, New Jersey, opposite the Palisades Amusement Park. He was the director. With my winnings plus what I had saved and some other money we borrowed, we invested about $14,000. The theater was in a building owned by the restaurant next door, and we operated it as a dinner theater. We should have had enough money to see us through a year, but we were badly undercapitalized and went out of business in five months.

For a while after that I worked at the St. Marks Theater in Manhattan's East Village, but the pay was modest—barely enough to live on. So I decided to get a regular job—the first real job I ever had—and I went to an employment agency. I had my college degree, some unusual experience which showed managerial capacity—and I was a terrific hearts player. The chick at the agency asked if I could type. I could, but not well enough for a business office. She was very disturbed with me and let me know I had a lot of crust even to look for a job. It was the same old story, the living example of all you hear about. She said, "You can't type, take shorthand, or work a switchboard. I don't know what you expect me to do for you," but she took a last look at all the information I had given her. Nothing pleased her until she noticed I had worked for two summers in the library at Northwestern. That was the only thing she could find that made any sense to her. It had been just a few hours a week for pin money and basically involved taking books off the cart and putting them on the shelves, but she had two openings for library trainees and sent me on an interview for one of them—at the American Cancer Society. I wound up there for the next ten years—more or less all of my twenties and a piece of my thirties.

As a bibliographer I worked on a lot of projects for Dr. Roald N. Grant, editor of the society's journal. When the woman who was managing editor left, I thought of asking for the job, but before I could work up the nerve they hired someone from the outside. When he left after two years, I asked for the job and got it. It mainly involved rewriting articles doctors sent in—putting them into English. I had had no doubt I could do that. I knew a lot about medicine by then and a lot about cancer. I didn't think it would be a problem, and it wasn't, but I was concerned about the original writing. Dr. Grant knew that, because we had talked about it, and it was he who taught me to write. He kept telling me, "If you can think, you can write." He would show me samples of writing he thought were good. One was a letter, and it became my model. It was a letter of introduction Dr. John Enders, the Nobel Prize-winning virologist, had written to tell Dr. Grant about a young man and his work and why Dr. Grant should be interested in helping him to get a grant to pursue his work. The clarity of that letter was astonishing. Dr. Grant said, "You see. He knows what he wants to say. He understands research. He understands virology. He understands everything he's writing about, and he doesn't mind my knowing it."

I enjoyed the technical writing. It was easy for me, and I was good at it, but eventually it started to annoy me that I didn't get to put my name on anything. I wrote for others who put their names on the articles, or they weren't signed at all. I used to write the editorials, but it was a physician who signed them, because who cared what I thought. Plus, I ran into the fem-lib thing. Dr. Grant died in 1969, and the next person I reported to was not the same quality of man. When I went into his office to talk about something to do with the magazine, he would talk about my dress or things like that. He did it in a way that made it clear he wasn't about to talk business with me. He wasn't trying to make a pass. It was just that I as a woman was a lesser mortal in his eyes. It didn't bother me at first, but then an interesting thing happened.

My assistant was a radical woman and very strong in her opinions, one of which was that women are just as good as men. I wasn't of that opinion at the time—mainly because I was reading a lot of good novels, and they all happened to be written by men. The Brontës really didn't measure up to Henry James and Charles Dickens, and no one ever had told me how good Jane Austen was. So my assistant and I would argue—until she gave me a copy of *Middlemarch*, by George Eliot. It totally threw me. It was an astonishing book, and its impact was enormous. There's no way to tell how much it meant to me. It probably was the most important thing that ever happened to me in terms of affecting the way I thought about things.

I realized that my way of thinking had been all wrong. Until I felt that, the comments about my dress didn't bother me. But once it got through to me, I couldn't hack that guy anymore. When he talked about how nice my dress was, it infuriated me. I literally wanted to pick up his desk and hit him with it. Plus, I wanted to make more money, at least as much as the man who had the job before I did. He had made about $3,000 a year more for doing the same job—and not as well. Three months after I took over the job, the magazine was on time for the first time in fourteen years, and I upped it from an average of sixty-two to seventy-four pages. So, thanks to George Eliot, I started looking for another job and wound up at *Drug Therapy* magazine.

It was entirely different there—a real pressure job, which I had wanted all along, and the challenge was wonderful. It was a small staff, and what you did made a difference and was noticed. I worked hard and, from assistant editor, became associate editor, senior editor, and finally editor. Then after a while I started to feel the same as I had at the American Cancer Society. I knew that as a woman I would have to be more extraordinary than I was to really be a success; that as long as I was working for other people I would not be signing my own work and would be working for less money than a man would make. I decided I had gone as far as I wanted to go there, although there were other things I could have done. They had offered me a managerial job on the publishing side, not on the editorial staff, but I really didn't want that. I had worked on some projects the magazine's advertising agency promoted, and I watched those guys. It was incredible. That's when I realized American businessmen don't really do business. They're not even interested in money. They are working out a complex tribal rite, and the money is just like shells or beads. I didn't want to waste my time with that, and decided I would find another way. That's when, still working at *Drug Therapy*, I began writing my three pages a night.

The Killing Gift made a lot of money, and when it did I decided to make a lot more money. My publisher, G.P. Putnam's, suggested I do a novel based on the newspaper accounts of the deaths of twin brothers, doctors. That led to my second book. Jack Geasland was senior editor at *Drug Therapy*, and a friend suggested to him that he write a novel based on the same accounts. That happened on the exact same day my publisher had mentioned it to me. As soon as Jack and I discovered this, we decided to collaborate on *Twins*. When we got our advance from Putnam's I quit *Drug Therapy*. He quit a month later. We had a tight deadline and knew we couldn't do the book and work too. It was just too much. As it was, we missed our deadline by six months. We had at least two false starts. We did outlines for stories we never wrote. It was a horrendous story, a brutal book, and I really was knocked out when I finished it. But the writing was all there, and it turned out much better than I thought it would.

Now I think I would like to write a really great book, but that's a bad motive. It's not a clear one. Wanting to write a good book is not a good reason to write a book. If you've got a story you want to tell, you should tell it, and that's the best reason. It's in deciding the way you're going to tell it that you ask yourself the other questions.

Writing comes easy to me because I have clear in my mind the thoughts I want to express and I express them directly. There have been times when what I was writing was going well and I just hated doing it. It was work, and it was annoying. Toward the end of writing *The Killing Gift*, it was desperation. I wanted to get it finished. All my time went into the rewriting. But usually I like writing when it goes well. If you don't, chances are you don't have a clear idea of what you want to write or you truly don't want to write at all. If you find it continually a problem, then you're just kidding yourself.

Daniel Yankelovich

PUBLIC OPINION ANALYST

A nationally recognized expert in the psychology of public attitudes, Daniel Yankelovich is president of the attitude research firm of Yankelovich, Skelly and White. He was born in Boston and educated at Harvard and the Sorbonne. He is research professor of psychology at New York University and visiting professor of psychology in the graduate faculty of the New School for Social Research. His other activities include serving as president of the Public Agenda Foundation, which he founded, and as a member of the boards of Common Cause, Work in America Institute, and the Institute for World Order. He is a special adviser to the Aspen Institute, a member of the Visiting Committee for the Department of Sociology at Harvard, and a member of the Council on Foreign Relations.

I backed into the field of the psychology of public attitudes somewhat by accident, due initially to projects I happened to get involved in as a graduate student while working to save money to study in Europe. I had no early interest in the study of large communities, for during my youth I was not aware that it existed as a general field.

My early background was somewhat chaotic. My mother died when I was eight. So I didn't know her very well. My father, who was born in Russia, came to the United States in the early years of the century. He worked and struggled and finally earned enough money to buy a few buildings in Boston, which he managed until he lost them during the Depression. The combination of that loss and the trauma of my mother's death during the Depression caused the breakup of our family—there were three children—and I lived thereafter in a series of foster homes.

During my high school years, when I attended the Boston Latin School, I thought I might become a musician. I played the flute and performed in various orchestras in Boston, but I spent most of my non-school hours working to help support myself—at an average wage of thirty-five cents an hour. My high school education consisted largely of mathematics and languages—Latin, German, and French—with a smattering of history and physics in the senior year. While it served a useful purpose as a kind of discipline or drill, it was not stimulating intellectually.

Private reading provided some relief. I was a compulsive reader and read everything I could get my hands on. Some of my jobs, such as night watchman and elevator operator, left plenty of time for reading. I read all the fiction I could, along with contemporary books on what was going on in the country politically and pop types of things on psychology and philosophy. I would take out as many books as the library allowed, read them, bring them back, and take out another batch. I had no systematic approach, but some fairly

Daniel Yankelovich: I was a compulsive reader and read everything I could get my hands on. Some of my jobs, such as night watchman and elevator operator, left plenty of time for reading.

good books did occasionally fall into my hands.

Harvard was a tonic for the spirit after the Boston Latin School. I found the intellectual experience mind-blowing, and the subject matter fell in with my own private, groping pursuits. I found philosophy, political science, and psychology most congenial, and I chose to major in philosophy, with a view to teaching at the university. At the end of my freshman year in 1943 I turned eighteen and was drafted into the Army. After basic training in Georgia I was assigned to the Army Corps of Engineers and went overseas, serving in France, Belgium, and Germany.

I found myself in the same situation as a lot of other GIs at the end of the war in Europe. Under the "point system," we were eligible to return home, but there weren't enough ships to take us all. So I entered a university program the Army had set up to keep the GIs out of mischief. One course in French language and civilization at the University of Grenoble in the south of France was open to soldiers who spoke a smattering of French. There was just a handful of us who took it, and it was a dramatic and welcome change after three years of soldiering.

When I returned to Harvard after the Army I gravitated toward the social sciences in order to round out my understanding of social philosophy, which, as it was taught at Harvard, tended to be overly abstract and somewhat empty of substantive content. Harvard had a social relations department which combined various aspects of social psychology, sociology, and social anthropology. It was a basic social science orientation. I found the work extremely interesting because of the breadth of its interdisciplinary approach. After I got my degree in 1948 I was appointed Rantoul Scholar in Clinical Psychology and stayed on at Harvard to pursue graduate studies. It was during this period that I received my first practical experience in studying the relationships between institutions and people.

The Massachusetts Institute of Technology, just down the road from Harvard, was concerned about the emotional stresses on veterans who, like myself, had returned to college after World War II.

These tensions exploded into a number of drop-outs, nervous break-downs, and even suicides. The MIT administration wondered if its policies and practices were exacerbating the situation in any way and if there was some way to alleviate it. As a psychologist-in-training I was given a part-time job working in a very subsidiary position on that project. It helped lay the groundwork for my eventual involvement in the field of studying how institutions and their policies affect people's lives. During that study some of the psychologists working on the same floor in MIT's industrial relations department consulted with me on some tests they were doing in pretesting consumer products and advertising.

Toward the end of my graduate studies, having saved enough money from these assignments, I took a leave from Harvard to go to Europe for a few years and continue my studies at the Sorbonne in Paris. I stayed there until my savings and GI benefits ran out. Then I found a free-lance job in Paris and worked for about nine months for the Economic Cooperation Administration under the Marshall Plan's Labor and Labor Information divisions. In a general sense, that represented my third experience in analyzing the relationship between an institution and the people it involved—in this case, the United States government, or at least an aspect of its policy, and the non-Communist trade unions of Europe. The government wanted to find ways to strengthen the free trade unions against the pressures of the Communist trade unions. In that assignment I traveled through-out Europe interviewing the heads of unions and compiling and analyzing their views regarding U.S. government policies.

When I came back to the United States I decided not to go into university teaching. This decision had been forming for a long time. I felt I simply did not know enough about my subject to teach it to other people. Since my interest was the relationship between the individual and society, I felt it wasn't healthy to go from being a student—with my knowledge almost totally book-oriented—to teaching without having the feel and the touch and the smell of what the society was actually like. Had my field of interest been mathematics or physics I might not have had that feeling, because one can teach such subjects without having firsthand experience as a practitioner.

Having decided not to return to Harvard, at least not right away, I did not feel there was much for me in Boston either. It was the early 1950s, and Boston offered considerably fewer opportunities than it does today. So I gravitated to New York because it seemed more ripe with possibilities. I started to cast about for a job in market research. With my training in psychology and my several work experiences, I knew of no other professional field where my background would be applicable.

After several interviews I received an offer from the industrial design firm of Nowland and Schladermundt. Roger Nowland, the head of the firm, already had begun to develop what he called "predesign research." It had become evident to him in his work of designing consumer and industrial products that designers knew engineering and aesthetics but were quite remote from the users' interests and needs. He felt that the people involved in the predesign research were providing him with data in which he wasn't interested—demographic data about users' ages, incomes, brand preferences, and the like. It was perfectly adequate market research information but not particularly useful for his designers. He wanted a fresh approach, which I certainly was able to bring to bear since I knew almost nothing about market research. So I went to work as a project director for Nowland and Schladermundt.

I structured a new research program. That feature of the firm's work soon caught on and became quite successful, but then a serious business conflict arose. There were some clients with the firm who liked the design work but who were not interested in paying extra for the predesign research, and there were other companies who started to come to the firm because of the research. Among them were those who took the findings elsewhere to have the design work done. This caused some internal tension, and in 1955 the firm split up. Roger Nowland continued the predesign research activity as

Nowland and Company. He moved it to Greenwich, Connecticut, and I went with him as research director.

He and I became very close and worked well together, but by 1958 I found myself in disagreement with some of the firm's personnel policies. When there was a lot of work, people were hired. When business dropped off, people were let go. It seemed to me it should have been possible to manage the firm in such a way as to eliminate the peaks and valleys or, at the very least, to keep the group together in bad times as well as good, since the main asset in a firm of this sort is the people. I felt it was futile to hire and train people who would then be let go at the first sign of an economic decline. That was bad not only for the people who were let go but for those who stayed, because they had no sense of cohesiveness, of building something together.

There was a reluctance, too, to take some of the gifted professional people and bring them more closely into the management of the firm, which I felt was indispensable. Roger Nowland agreed with me in principle, but, because of commitments he had to other people, he didn't feel he could make the changes necessary to build the kind of organization I strongly felt was needed. So with great reluctance I left and opened my own firm

I started with no capital to speak of. We were very small but received enough business and enough attention to get off to a good start. There was at the time a number of large, important market research firms with capabilities we didn't have. They were able to undertake large-scale studies among national cross-sections of consumers. By virtue of our limitations of size and resources we sought out all the difficult problems no one else wanted to tackle.

As it turned out, that served us in good stead. Major American corporations were beginning to realize the full importance and usefulness of market research and wanted more control over it. They felt that by doing more of the conventional research in-house they could maintain control and save money as well. Therefore a great many companies began to establish their own internal departments. As a result, the major market research firms suffered a tremendous loss of business. It was a perfect example of a field being hurt by its own success. Since of necessity we had positioned ourselves in the less conventional part of the field—in the motivational and psychological areas—we not only were not hurt but began to get even more business. As our business grew, we were able to expand our capabilities.

Since I had been trained as a social scientist I always had the desire to broaden the base of the firm into the social sciences as well as the market research area. The opportunity to do so presented itself in the mid-1960s. At that time there were signs that something important was happening to the values of college youth—the most rapidly expanding part of the population. The firm had reached a sufficient size and become a significant enough factor in the field that the Institute for Life Insurance asked me to prepare a presentation on the subject for their annual meeting in 1965, summarizing for the chief executive officers of the various life insurance companies what was happening to the nation's young people.

In the course of preparing for that talk, in doing the research and study analysis for it, I realized that something quite significant was taking place, and after I gave the talk I decided to pursue the subject. *Fortune* magazine agreed to sponsor a full-scale study of youth and their attitudes and values. That project led to a similar study the following year for CBS and then to a series of annual studies sponsored by the JDR 3rd Fund and a number of other foundations. By then I knew we were looking at a very important historical situation. Our studies on youth were published in book form in 1970, 1971, and 1973. They described how the new values incubating on the nation's campuses were beginning to transform the country's social environment.

Our market research activities fully substantiated the fact that the social environment was indeed changing. Ford and General Motors, for instance, became aware that changes outside their own backyards were affecting their business—that it wasn't what each other was doing but larger and more puzzling changes in the character of American culture. We began to receive more and more assignments to analyze and develop an understanding about what was happening in the social environment. After a number of those studies, it was readily apparent that the changes were universal and had broad implications—beyond any single company or industry. In response to that, we developed a research program called the "Yankelovich Monitor" through which we offered to undertake annual studies to track the year-by-year social changes taking place in the country. We then went out and found companies to help defray the cost of research by co-sponsoring the studies.

Since 1965 we have built up a number of social research programs and a body of knowledge that is probably unique about what is happening in this country—beginning with the student movement on campus and the various social movements, including the civil rights and consumer movements, the women's movement, the changing work ethic, the political climate, and the spread of new values. It has been developed through a whole series of research programs, each of which has looked at changes in the society from a different point of view. The opportunity to do this, to understand not only what is going on but why, is compelling and fascinating. By being close to the center of what is going on we have been able, in varying degrees, to bring that knowledge into the domain of policy decisions—not only those of our clients but public policy decisions as well.

While retaining and strengthening our market research activities, our firm has developed a strong identification as a monitor of social change—not just in collecting the data but in analyzing and under-standing its meaning, illuminating what was and is happening so as to guide policy. I don't think anyone can understand what goes on in the minds of 200 million Americans without studying it factually, instead of making intuitive guesses—projecting one's own values.

My training is somewhat different from that of many other people in the field. I always have been drawn to what things mean—not just collecting data but understanding the meaning behind that data. I feel I was lucky to have entered the field at a comparatively early stage in its development and at a time when the changing nature of our society made our work so relevant. At the same time, I have tried to shape new methods and approaches for studying such change so that they are, I hope, adding something to our self-understanding.